THE YOUNG MALE FIGURE

frontispiece:

DEGAS, HILAIRE GERMAIN EDGAR
1834–1917, French
Spartan Boys (detail), 1860
The National Gallery, London

Degas was one of the early, great modern Impressionists. He often combined classical themes with his own feelings for reality. Thus in this painting, which is a detail of the whole painting called *Young Spartan Girls Challenging Spartan Boys,* this group of awkward, slender, naked boys defiantly faces a group of clothed young girls in a game, while in the background the elder Greeks are engaged in conversation. The impressionistic rendering of these immature youths possesses a strong esoteric appeal.

THE YOUNG MALE FIGURE

IN PAINTINGS, SCULPTURES, AND DRAWINGS
FROM ANCIENT EGYPT TO THE PRESENT

BRANDT AYMAR

CROWN PUBLISHERS, INC., NEW YORK

Also by Brandt Aymar

A PICTORIAL TREASURY OF THE MARINE MUSEUMS OF THE WORLD
CRUISING IS FUN
THE COMPLETE CRUISER
GUIDE TO BOATMANSHIP, SEAMANSHIP AND SAFE BOAT HANDLING
CRUISING GUIDE

Edited by Brandt Aymar

TREASURY OF SNAKE LORE
THE PERSONALITY OF THE CAT
THE DECK CHAIR READER
THE PERSONALITY OF THE BIRD
THE PERSONALITY OF THE HORSE
THE PERSONALITY OF THE DOG

With Edward Sagarin

A PICTORIAL HISTORY OF THE WORLD'S GREAT TRIALS

LIBRARY OF CONGRESS CATALOG CARD NUMBER: 78-127501
PRINTED IN THE UNITED STATES OF AMERICA
PUBLISHED SIMULTANEOUSLY IN CANADA BY
GENERAL PUBLISHING COMPANY LIMITED

CONTENTS

Foreword

The purpose of this book is to present the young male figure through the ages of art history from ancient Egypt of about 2500 B.C. to the present, a span of nearly 4,500 years. Though a reasonable assumption would be that in all these years thousands of representations of the young male figure must have been created from which to choose, surprisingly enough, once the many statues of ancient Greece and their Roman copies have been excluded, there are relatively few. Thus a great deal of research was required to compile this collection of the young male figure, whose ages run from childhood to young manhood.

At the outset it is only fair to state what this book is not. It does not attempt to include every period of art history of every civilization and culture. It is selective on several grounds: the author's own personal choices, the physical size of the book, and the intent to present the young male figure only when he has esthetic appeal. Certain periods of art history are thus automatically excluded. For example, when Christian art of the Middle Ages superseded Greek and Roman art, sculptural nudity was banned, and the young male figures, carved mainly as parts of church edifices, were so full draped and so grotesquely featured that they lost their esthetic appeal. Therefore they have been omitted from this book. Similarly, most Oriental art, other than the figure of the young Buddha and his followers, is devoid of the young male figure as the center of interest. In our own twentieth century, as soon as representational painting gave way to Abstraction, the young male figure vanished from the artist's canvas and from this book as well.

Within the limits of this book's concept there are nearly three hundred examples of the young male figure in art through the ages. All the sculptures are nude, as would be expected, since 90 percent of all sculptural figures are of nudes. Also, since most creative artists usually drew their preliminary figure sketches in the nude, most of the drawings in this work are so depicted. The paintings are equally divided between portraiture and the young male nude in art.

Each of the six main sections is introduced by a concise résumé of the political and social backgrounds in which each of the particular periods or schools of art flourished, along with the names of the famous artists represented in this volume. The text which accompanies each illustration first gives the pertinent physical facts of the work, followed by a short commentary relating the artist and his work to his times and influences. It is intended to place the work in its proper perspective and not act as a detailed critique.

Most of the famous artists who painted, sculptured, or drew the young male figure are represented in this book. I would like to thank the directors and curators of the art museums from all parts of the world for their very gracious cooperation in supplying my requests for these photographs of works in their collections.

BRANDT AYMAR

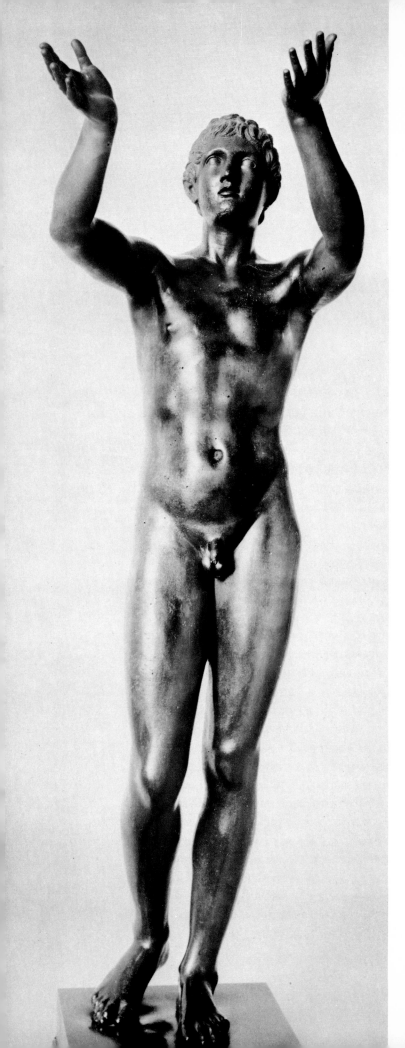

CLASSIC GREEK
Late fourth century B.C.
Praying Boy
Copy of a work by Boida, son of Lysippus
Bronze, ht. 50⅜ in.
Staatliche Museen, Berlin

Lysippus changed the Greek design of
his day by making his youths slenderer
and their heads smaller. In this way they
looked taller, as in this pose of a praying
youth. The body is softer and the thighs
and legs smoother. Thus the three greats
of the fourth century—Scopas,
Praxiteles, and Lysippus—carved and
influenced the creation of the finest
sculptures in all art history.

PART I

In Antiquity

The heyday of the young male in art occurred in an era from 461 to 429 B.C., known as the Golden Age of Greek history. During these few years the art of sculpture reached its highest pinnacle and gave the world the classic, slender Greek male figure that has not been surpassed in over two thousand years. How did it happen that this particular small span of history was chosen to be endowed with such fame? Naturally it did not happen overnight. In fact, this classic male figure was the result of development over many hundreds of years, and it came into being at the precise era it did through a fortuitous combination of cultural factors that were religious, political, economic, social, and psychological.

Art history began in prehistoric times with the first cave wall paintings. Since these were simple line sketches depicting characters and elementary actions such as hunting and farming, they are of little concern with the young male in art. But about the fourth millennium in Mesopotamia, the cradle of civilization, we come across many ancient pottery figurines that bear a close resemblance to the young male.

As the various ancient Egyptian dynasties succeeded one another, representation in statuary of the human body became far more pronounced, but along stringently confining lines. As subject matter, only the kings and the priests, the god representatives on earth, were carved. They were always portrayed in stiff and stylized poses, and for a purpose. These statues represented their god-given authority over the lands and the peoples, and must, therefore, be presented in awe-inspiring, oversized forms designed to preserve their dignity and omnipotence. It was totalitarian art in the extreme, yet these figures did possess a limited degree of individual personality, even as far back as 2500 B.C. One of the best examples of a young male Egyptian in art is found in the head of the teen-age king, Tutankhamen, who died about 1350 B.C.

It was entirely natural that Greek works of art were influenced to a large extent by these hundreds of years of creation of Egyptian statues. From 1000 to 500 B.C., known as the Archaic period, the Greek artists adhered closely to the Egyptian techniques of rigid frontal formality. These early young Greek male figures were known as Apollos or Kouroi. Closely associated with the Greek gods, whom they represented, they were used as religious adornments on temples, both standing alone in the round and in relief to decorate

1

the walls of sacred buildings. They were carved simply and uncluttered, both halves of the frontal appearance exactly alike, arms held rigid and close to the sides, the left foot always in front of the right one, and a wiglike hairdress on the head—in all, a very close cousin to their Egyptian prototypes.

Yet there were differences and new developments. Faint glimmers of human anatomy began to appear, definite muscles and sinews. Most important of all, these young men in art were now always nude. Freed from the rule of tyrants and kings, the Greek artist, creating in an environment of individual freedom, literally shed all garments from his figures as he began to renounce the old authoritative concepts. Now he could depict what he saw the young male to be, and what he saw was anything but the solemn stereotypes of previous civilizations.

The tempo of change accelerated as Greek art passed from the Archaic period and late in the sixth century B.C. entered the Classic period. Now the young male in sculpture began to assume the beauty and prowess he so well displayed in real life. While the remnants of the Archaic style lingered on for a few years, the stiffness began to abate. The statues were still used as parts of religious edifices, but now, in addition, the young male in art was given wider latitude: he was carved as handles for serving utensils and other utilitarian objects, and he was used as an important personage in vase painting, which had its brief vogue during the next several centuries. He was fast approaching the perfection that was to characterize the Golden Age of Greek sculpture.

It is now necessary, as the beginning of the fifth century B.C. approached, to look at the stage to which the civilization of the Greek states had progressed and to see how the cultural environment made times ripe for the coming of the Golden Age. On the military front, peace had at last come to the Greek lands in 479 B.C. after they had twice turned back Persian invaders. First the Persian forces were soundly defeated in the Battle of Marathon in 490 B.C., then their naval forces were demolished at Salamis in 480 B.C., and a year later they were defeated at Mykale. Having no longer to fear invasion by the Persian forces, the Greek states united in a federation in which Athens took the lead over Sparta. During the just-ended wars many of the Greek temples had been destroyed along with much of the statuary. At last, in peace, a period of rebuilding and creating new works in an atmosphere of liberty began.

On the political scene the signs were equally propitious for the advancement of art and culture. This was the age of Pericles, the greatest of all Greek statesmen, who established the first democratic society in the history of the world and instituted numerous democratic reforms. Of course, all this applied to a minority of the population, the Athenian citizens, who alone could vote, but the Greek world was now one where individual liberty was encouraged and cherished. It is easy to see how beneficial such an atmosphere was for the encouragement of the Greek artists in their pursuit for perfection of the human form. Phidias, the greatest sculptor of the Golden Age, was designated to decorate the newly built Parthenon. The noted playwrights Aeschylus and Sophocles were realizing the height of their popularity.

The Athenians' attitude toward religion was another important contributing factor to the arts. The people were free to worship what gods they wanted, and there were many of them. To the Greeks these gods were but immortal human beings, beautiful and perfect. Thus, when sculptors carved young males they endowed them with all the godlike qualities the people revered so highly. The results were beautifully idealized nude forms, free from human blemishes, handsome and heroic as the Greek gods themselves. Religion and philosophy joined in the worship of beauty, for such beauty was truth itself, the attainment of which was the utmost goal.

In the social and sexual aspects of Greek society of this period lies another basic reason why the young male was so worshiped in art. Theirs was an openly bisexual society in which love of one's wife was directed toward the home and the raising of a family, not to be confused with the love of young boys by older males. Each had its proper place in the orderly pursuit of daily living, and the latter was equally important to the physical and spiritual life of the Athenian as was marriage and the procreation of the species. It was no wonder that the idolization of the young male resulted in magnificent nude male statuary which flowered everywhere.

That male sculptures were always nude was not solely the result of a homosexually oriented society. Male nudity was taken for granted by the Greeks in the very nature of the educational system of that era. Greek culture was comparatively new, and their historic past consisted mainly of the Homeric legends. These formed the basics of learning taught in the schools, together with philosophical discussions and rhetoric. Equal emphasis was placed on physical education and the development of a beautiful physique. Participation in sports and in athletic contests was required of all young boys until they reached the age of eighteen and became eligible for military service. Religious festivals consisted of games and contests dedicated to the gods, the most famous being the Pythian games at Delphi. The young men competed in wrestling, running, jumping, throwing the javelin and the discus. At none of these Athenian events were women allowed to be spectators, much less to participate. Thus, it was perfectly natural for all the young men to take part in these events in the nude. The crowds of spectators came to cheer the victors and to worship the physical beauty with which these youths were endowed. They were indeed young gods to behold.

The religion of the Athenians taught that they should emulate the gods since the gods were simply humans endowed with immortal life, who still behaved like humans. Thus, the practice of homosexual love was part of the lives of these gods: Zeus, the king of the gods, loved his Ganymede, Apollo his Hyacinth, and there were many other noted liaisons. These religious and social customs of the citizens were basic to the achievements of their artists. The sculptors carved nude monuments in praise of the victors of the athletic contests. They extolled the beauty of the young male, transforming the purely physical into idealistic harmony and perfection of compact form. These statues were symbolic of the Greek belief that beauty and goodness went hand in hand, and to enjoy both was indeed the final attainment of truth itself.

This then was the situation in Athens that enabled Greek Classic art to reach its highest peak in the second half of the fifth century. A short transition period soon came to an end, during which Apollos were still being carved, such as the magnificent youth found in the sea near Piombino, Italy. But the *Youth* attributed to Kritios shows a marked difference, with its much more subtle contours, greater anatomical details, and, above all, its closer representation of the ideal Greek youth. It was Polycleitus who carved this ideal youth to such perfect proportions that his works have forever stood as a shining example of the finest of the Golden Age. Unfortunately most original Greek sculptures have perished, and we must learn about them through Roman copies. Yet enough originals are extant for us to appreciate the esthetic heights reached in this all too brief age, which came to an abrupt end with the beginning of the Peloponnesian War of 431–404 B.C.

A long civil war ensued between Athens and Sparta, which took its toll of Athenian artistic achievements. Instead of spending money on temple building, all available funds went into military activities. Temple building and statue carving came virtually to a halt. For the next fifty years after the war ended there was little innovation in the art of sculpture. What was carved took on a certain refinement and decorativeness, but nothing revolutionary occurred until the middle of the fourth century when a new wave of artistic creativity swept into Athens. Once again Greek art was to reach another plateau of sculptural perfection.

The time of this new outburst of cultural energy became known as the Age of Praxiteles, Scopas, and Lysippus. This trio established a new approach to the young male in sculpture that was to influence other artists for years to come. In contrast to the flawless, idealized heroic youths of the Golden Age, the statues fashioned by these three artistic giants became more realistic, more human, more representative of the true nude forms of youth. The bodies were softer, smoother, and with more curves. Features assumed more expressiveness. Moods in which the statues were carved became more relaxed. Here was the young male as he actually appeared in life without the heroics of the past.

Conquest and war soon again interfered with art progress, except this time it was the Greeks who under Philip II of Macedonia and his illustrious son, Alexander the Great, set out and managed to conquer the civilized world, including Persia and Egypt. This period lasted until the death of Alexander in 323 B.C., by which time the last period of Greek art, the Hellenistic, was being ushered in. Alexander had reached as far east as India, and everywhere he and his victorious armies went he Hellenized the lands he conquered. Thus Greek culture, heretofore confined to Athens and the neighboring states, was spread far and wide. The immediate effect was that Athens ceased to be the art center of the world and was replaced by such eastern centers as Pergamon, Rhodes, and Alexandria.

Art became international. In addition to classical Greek works still being produced, other works took on a baroque realism and a rococo decorativeness. Figures and groups were now carved in every different pose and attitude. The emphasis was on motion and activity: a young jockey from Artemis literally leaping out into space, the famous Hellenistic wrestlers twisted into a terrifyingly complex huddle, the Borghese warrior hurtling his spear toward an invisible enemy, and on a quieter plane, but pulsating with rhythm, a young Nubian musician of the second to first centuries B:C.

With the rise of the Roman Empire and the subjugation of the Greek states and Egypt to the Roman rulers, artistic advancement came to a virtual standstill. The so-called

Greco-Roman period was one in which thousands of copies of earlier Greek works were made by Roman sculptors, but, except for busts of members of the Roman ruling class, little original carving was done. However, Roman art of the first, second, and third centuries A.D. did include some exquisitely carved sarcophagi, and their influence in portraiture was also felt at this time in Egypt in the wooden funerary plaques, which replaced the Egyptian tomb statuary.

The coming of Christianity sounded the death knell of further artistic progress and put an end to free expression in art works. Now the pagan works of the Greeks were replaced by Christian Byzantine art, to which the nude figure was anathema, as were any thoughts of the sexuality and sensuality of the human body itself. The role of well-robed saints predominated, while the naked young male in art receded into the Dark Ages of medievalism and mediocrity, where he would slumber for more than one thousand years.

MESOPOTAMIAN AND EGYPTIAN ART

Mankind's first-known paintings and drawings were scratched on the walls of caves and tombs of ancient Egyptian civilization. The figures of both humans and animals consisted of simple linear outlines. Since they do not represent our concept of the young male in art, none is included in this book. But as statues and elaborate tomb ornaments were carved in honor of the various Egyptian king-deities, the figures took on new dimensions, however stiff and formal. Our first young male in antiquity dates back to the fourth millennium and our first Egyptian statue to about 2500 B.C. or Dynasty V, and for all his formality he appears very human indeed.

MESOPOTAMIAN
Fourth millennium B.C., Al-'Ubaid period
Male Figurine
Terra-cotta, ht. 5½ in.
Baghdad Museum, Baghdad, Iraq

The religion of the inhabitants of
Mesopotamia in this millennium forbade
their artists to represent the human
figure in a purely lifelike way. Thus,
instead of a human face, they were
forced to resort to a weird snakelike
head. As with this figurine, the nude
male figure was always carved very thin,
in a standing position, and with clay
pellets about his shoulders. This is one
of the earliest representations of the
young male in art from a very early
period in the history of man.

EGYPTIAN
C. 2500 B.C.
Male Figure with Phallus Sheath
Diorite
The Brooklyn Museum
Brooklyn, New York

Perhaps this deity is from the Libyan
province in the West Delta, since he is
dressed in a typical costume of the
Egyptian's Libyan neighbors. Both the
knotted belt and the sheath surrounding
the penis are found in many of the
statues of this very early period. In his
right hand the god holds a knife.

EGYPTIAN. C. 1350 B.C. *Head of Tutankhamen*
Cover of a Canopic jar from his tomb. Alabaster, ht. 9⅜ in.
Egyptian Museum, Cairo

King Tut was the famous teen-age king who briefly reigned and died young about the middle of the fourteenth century B.C. His powerful and mysterious image is captured for posterity in this softly carved piece of alabaster. It was found in his burial chamber along with jars containing his vital organs. While sculptured along the formal straight planes of rigid Egyptian art, his face shows more emotion and personality than the usual carved deification of these rulers. The hawk and the snake in the middle of his forehead represent his rule over the twin kingdoms of Upper and Lower Egypt.

EGYPTIAN. C. 350–300 B.C. *Horus on Crocodiles.* Black steatite
The Brooklyn Museum, Brooklyn, New York

This stela, or cippus, represents the god Horus as a child. It was
considered a magic amulet to protect the wearer against the sting of
scorpions, the bite of poisonous snakes, and the influence of other
dangerous animals. In one hand the young god has a wild animal by
the horns; in the other, its tail. His expression is one of confidence in
the efficacy of his protective powers.

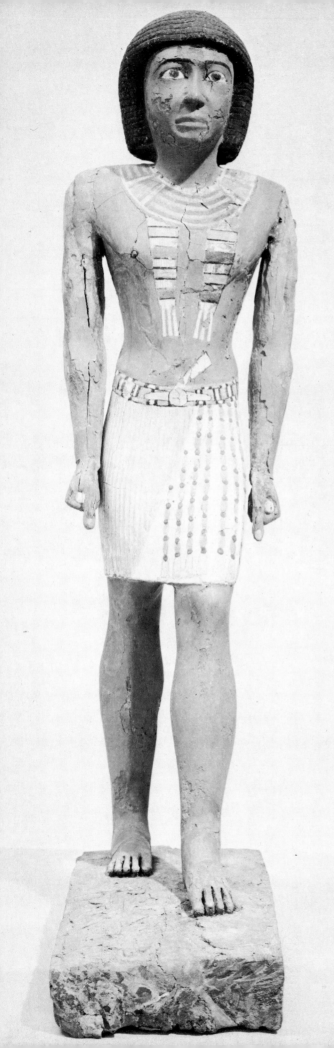

EGYPTIAN
C. 2420 B.C.
Methethy as a Young Man
Wood with painted gesso
The Brooklyn Museum
Brooklyn, New York

An important personage during the reign of King Unas, last king of Dynasty V, Methethy is here shown as a vigorous young man. He has assumed the traditional Egyptian striding pose, the stiff left foot ahead of an equally stiff right foot with arms straight down by his sides. This statue is from Saqqara, Old Kingdom.

10

ARCHAIC GREEK
615–600 B.C.
Kouros
Marble
The Metropolitan Museum of Art
New York, Fletcher Fund, 1932

A statue belonging to the Archaic period in Greek sculpture. It is one of the earliest of such sculptures known. It could almost be an Egyptian piece with its arms rigidly clinging to the sides of the body, its straight legs one in front of the other, its expressionless eyes indicating formality, and its wiglike hair. However, there is one important basic difference between this and the Egyptian art from which it sprang. This Greek statue is totally nude. It also begins to show muscular outlines. While still definitely archaic, it foreshadows the Golden Age of fifth-century-B.C. Greek sculpture. It is the beginning of the Greek culture's dedication to the beauty of the male nude.

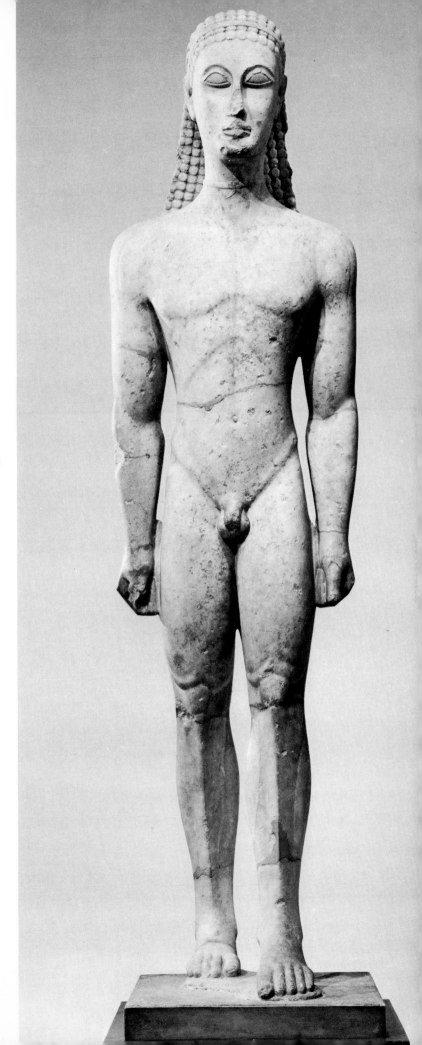

ARCHAIC GREEK. C. 510 B.C. *Athletes Wrestling*
Bas-relief from a pedestal. Marble, $12\frac{1}{2} \times 31\frac{1}{2}$ in.
National Museum, Athens

This wrestling match was typical of the intense Greek interest in sports.
During the last of the Archaic period many temples were built and
dedicated to the Greek gods. To ornament them sculptors carved scenes
in relief and in the round of male athletic activities. Since women were
not allowed to witness these games, the young males all participated
in the nude.

ARCHAIC GREEK. C. 510 B.C. *Youths Playing Ball*
Side of a sculptural base. Marble, $12\frac{5}{8} \times 31\frac{7}{8}$ in.
National Museum, Athens

Another sculptural panel of the same period. The nude young men are
here pictured enjoying themselves in a ball game. In order to develop
their bodies into beautiful physiques, the youths of Greece were urged
to partake often in athletic activities.

ARCHAIC GREEK. 520–510 B.C. *Grave Stele of a Helmeted Warrior*
National Museum, Athens

The striding figure was a favorite in Greek sculpture from early times,
especially of warriors. The two parts of the body are still not
coordinated, the upper one is facing the viewer, while the lower part
shows the side of the buttocks and thighs.

ARCHAIC GREEK. C. 500 B.C. *Patera Handle.* Bronze
Diameter of bowl 11¾ in., length of handle 7¾ in.
Royal Ontario Museum, Toronto

Even in their everyday utensils the Greeks used the male nude for
utilitarian purposes as in this handle for a shallow bowl. The figure
is still of the Archaic period, but now the body has been fashioned for
its usefulness. The young man is standing, feet together, on a ram's
head, and with uplifted arms is holding two rams back to back, to
which is connected the main part of the bowl. Such decorative utensils
were used in serving food and were found throughout the Greek world
of this period.

14

ARCHAIC GREEK
Early fifth century, B.C.
Apollo
Bronze, ht. 45¼ in.
Louvre Museum, Paris

This still Archaic statue of a youth was
found in the sea near Piombino, Italy.
Its stiffness is somewhat less than that of
the Apollo in the Metropolitan Museum
of Art, and the Egyptian influence on
Archaic Greek sculpture is beginning to
lessen.

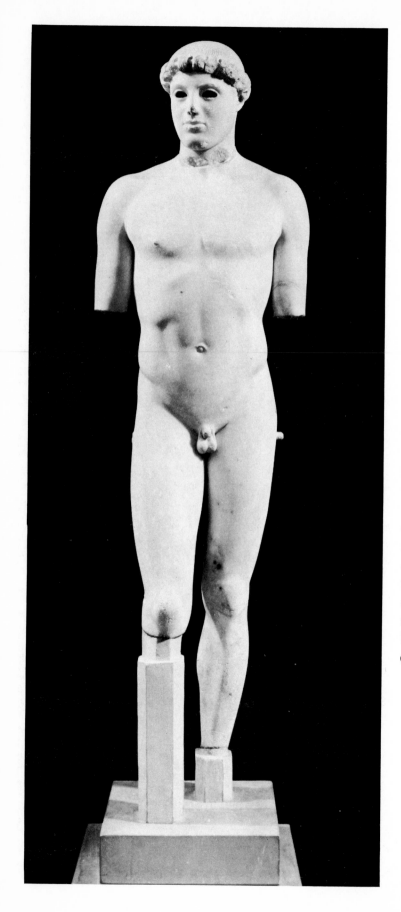

CLASSIC GREEK
C. 490 B.C. *Youth*
Attributed to Kritios
Marble, ht. 34½ in.
Acropolis Museum, Athens

A revolutionary change took place in
Greek sculpture during the first half of
the fifth century, as can be seen by
comparing the body of this youth with
those of the prior Archaic period. The
stiff symmetrical pose of Egyptian
inheritance is gone, the body has taken
on more natural curves, and the weight
is distributed more to one foot than
equally to both. The head is slightly
turned instead of being entirely frontal,
and the Archaic hairdo is gone. He
represents a healthy young athlete with
body proportions fulfilling the ideal
Greek requirements of this period.

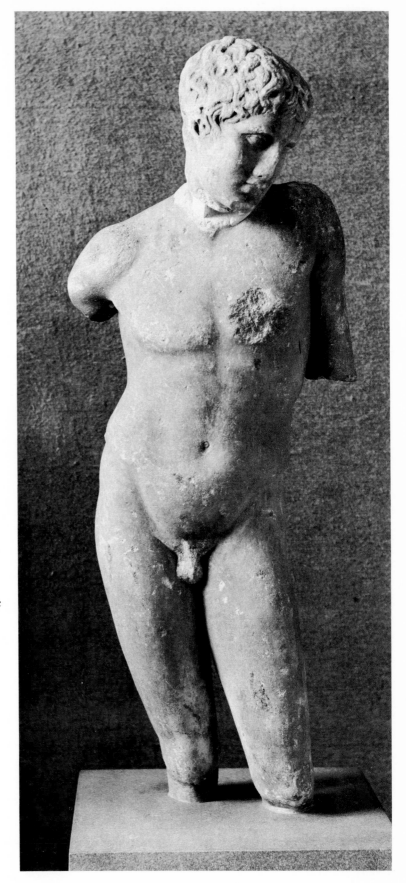

CLASSIC GREEK
Fifth century. *Narcissus*
Copy after Polycleitus
Fogg Art Museum, Harvard University
Cambridge, Massachusetts

Beginning with the fifth century Greek
sculpture took on more idealistic and
spiritual qualities. The pose of the body
was more elastic, as the curved body of
this young self-loving boy shows. The
head is bent well forward, and the glance
is downward. The stance is natural
and at ease.

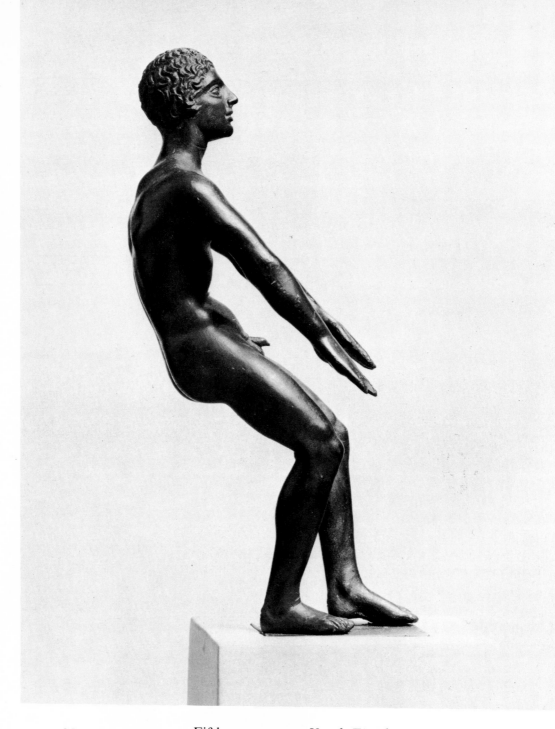

CLASSIC GREEK. Fifth century B.C. *Youth Finishing a Jump.* Bronze
The Metropolitan Museum of Art, New York, Rogers Fund, 1908

This statuette of an athlete was found in Tarentum. It is an excellent
example of the crouching figure, in which the Greek sculptors of this
period indulged. They now discovered they could carve the human form
in any number of different poses.

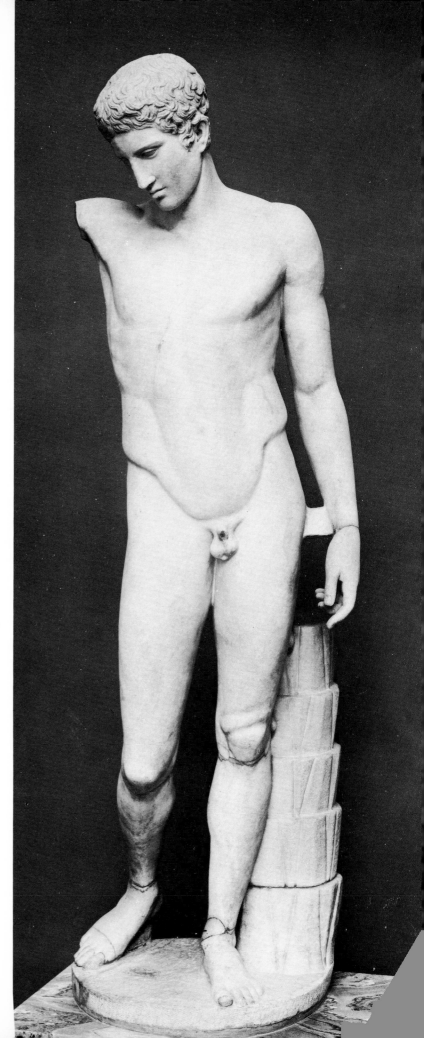

CLASSIC GREEK
450–440 B.C.
The "Westmacott Athlete"
Marble
British Museum, London

This statue of a boy, who was originally
placing a wreath on his head with his
missing hand, is a Roman copy of what
might possibly be an original Polycleitus.
The subject may very well be Kyniskos,
the boy boxer from Mantinea. It can be
identified in the way the right leg is
placed well to the rear and the foot
sideways, and in the excellent carving
of the pelvis.

CLASSIC GREEK
Late fifth century
Youth
Bronze, ht. 6¼ in.
William Rockhill Nelson Gallery of Art
Kansas City, Missouri, Nelson Fund

This youth is from Cumae and in style
shows the influence of Polycleitus. Since
both hands have holes in them, the boy
was probably holding some sort of
athletic equipment. His expression is
somewhat startling due to the sharply
horizontal eyebrows and the large eyes
with their pierced pupils.

CLASSIC GREEK. Late fifth century *Niobid*
Ny Carlsberg Glyptotek, Copenhagen

Here is one of the finest examples of a Greek reclining figure. The difficulty encountered in carving this figure was to correct naturally each part of the body so that it would present a harmonious whole without the stiffness of sculpture of the previous periods. Another difficulty was in achieving the rhythmic effect of the twist of the body between the upper portion and the legs. It could have been that this figure influenced Michelangelo in carving his *Dying Slave*.

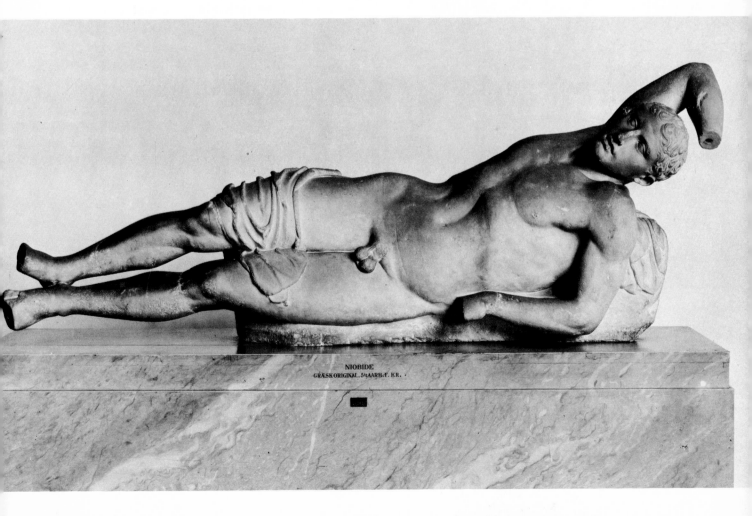

NIOBIDE
GRÆSK ORIGINAL. 5te AARH. F. KR.

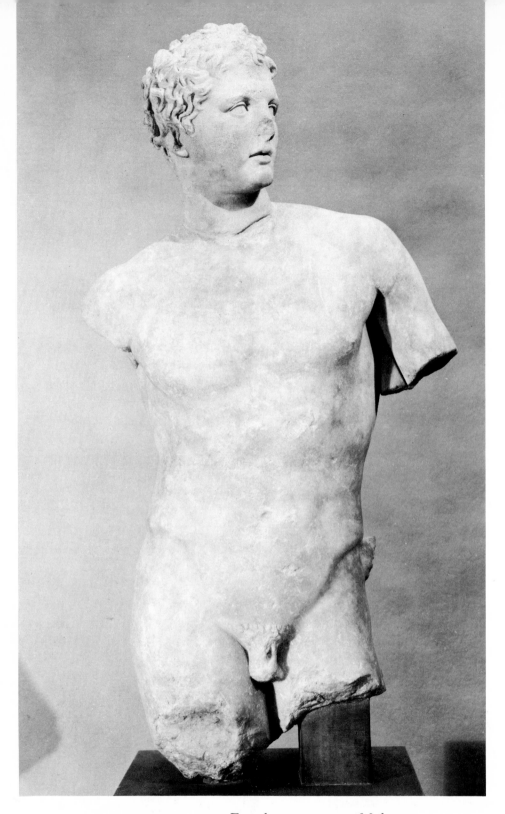

CLASSIC GREEK. Fourth century B.C. *Meleager*
Marble, in the style of Scopas, ht. 46 in.
Fogg Art Museum, Harvard University, Cambridge, Massachusetts

Little is known of Scopas' works, but this fine figure with deep-set eyes could very well be one of them. Whatever he did was imitated widely and set a new style of charm and delicacy, which characterized the greatest achievements of all Greek sculpture.

C. 343 B.C.
Hermes with the Infant Dionysos
Praxiteles
Olympia Museum, Athens

Here is a known original of the great
Greek sculptor Praxiteles and an example
of feminine delicacy in the new Greek
art of the fourth century. Like the Scopas
work, this statue exudes tenderness and
charm. The figure of Hermes is soft,
not heroic, gracious, not domineering,
comfortably relaxed, not stiff. He is
supporting the figure of the child
Dionysos, who is stretching out his arm
for something Hermes is holding. This
is the age when sensuous beauty in
Greek sculpture reached its height.

CLASSIC GREEK. Second half of fourth century B.C.
Head of a Young Man. Bronze. *National Museum, Athens*

This youthful statue was found in the Bay of Marathon after resting on
the bottom of the sea in a wrecked ship for 2,000 years. The close-up
of the head shows some of the vast changes which took place from fifth-
century features in order to create a much more natural appearance.
The sunken eyes are much more expressive, the mouth rounder and
more sensuous, the hair fuller and with more waves. This ideal beauty
was worshiped by Greek males.

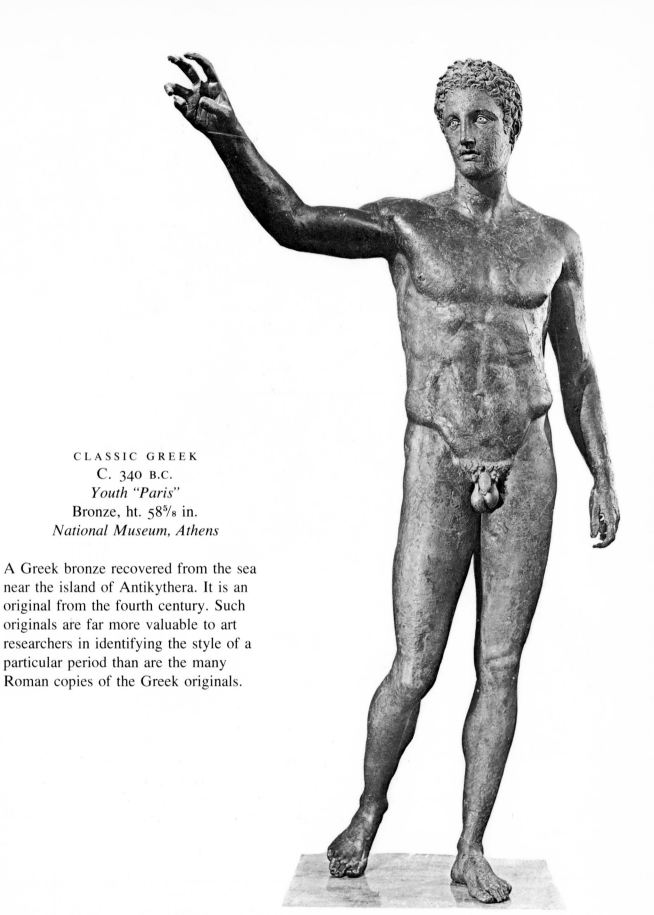

CLASSIC GREEK
C. 340 B.C.
Youth "Paris"
Bronze, ht. 58⅝ in.
National Museum, Athens

A Greek bronze recovered from the sea
near the island of Antikythera. It is an
original from the fourth century. Such
originals are far more valuable to art
researchers in identifying the style of a
particular period than are the many
Roman copies of the Greek originals.

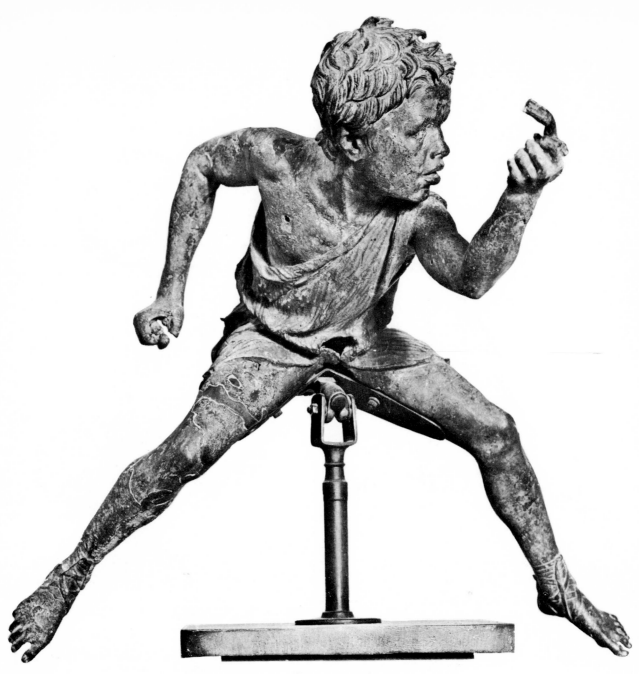

HELLENISTIC. Late second century. *Jockey*
Bronze, ht. 33⅛ in.
National Museum, Athens
A very dynamic Hellinistic work, this bronze was found in the sea off
Cape Artemision near Athens. During this particular period many
subject varieties were carved, especially action poses. This youthful,
exuberant jockey is astride his horse and urging him on with all the
skill at his command.

HELLENISTIC. *The Wrestlers*
Uffizi Galleries, Florence

This group is considered to be one of the finest examples of Greek
sculpture, especially of Hellenistic sculpture. The conquering athlete
has thrown his adversary to the ground and is still threatening him.
Each muscle bulges with effort, each vein pulsates with emotion. The
loser is still trying to get up and his expression is one of impotent
wrath, while the winner obviously is rejoicing in his victory. This Greek
masterpiece was brought to Rome in 1677.

HELLENISTIC. Second century B.C. *The Borghese Warrior*
Louvre Museum, Paris

This copy by Agasias, son of Dositheos, is dated from the first century
B.C., while authorities attribute the original to the Hellenistic second
century B.C. period. It is indicative of a stark realism of action with
which this period in Greek sculpture is associated. The detailed anatomy
and muscular tensions are extraordinary for such an era.

HELLENISTIC
Second to first centuries B.C.
Nubian Musician
Bronze, ht. 8 in.
Bibliothèque Nationale, Paris

A statuette of a completely charming and
sensuous young black boy that was found
in 1763 at Châlon-sur-Saône. He appears
to be deeply absorbed in what he is
playing, and his large lips and open
mouth show a certain sexual gratification
he is enjoying at this particular moment.

ETRUSCAN. Fourth to third century B.C.
Two Youths Carrying the Dead Body of a Companion
Bronze handle of a cista
The Metropolitan Museum of Art, New York, Rogers Fund, 1913

While defeated by the Romans in a war that began in the late sixth
century B.C. and lasted over 250 years, the Etruscans exerted a profound
influence on Roman art. Often nude figures, such as shown here, were
used to form a handle for the lid of a cista, a container for toilet
articles, just as the Greeks used such figures for handles on their
serving utensils.

30

CYPRIOTE. About fourth century B.C. *Temple Boy Holding Bird*
Limestone with traces of red paint
The Metropolitan Museum of Art, New York, Cesnola Collection

31

GRECO-ROMAN
100 B.C.–200 A.D.
Statue of a Boy
Pentelic marble, ht. 50¼ in.
Said to have been found in the Tiber
Museum of Fine Arts, Boston

This nude figure is of a boy about twelve
years old. He is standing with his weight
on his left leg and leaning forward, as
if about to run. His wavy hair is tied in
a knot on top. Because he looks so
feminine, one art critic refers to him as
a young Apollo, while another feels he
is a victorious boy athlete. This work
is a Roman copy of an original Greek
bronze.

GRECO-ROMAN
Fourth century B.C.
Young Satyr Pouring Wine
Praxiteles
Marble, ht. 5 ft.
Museo Archeologico Nazionale
Palermo, Sicily

A Roman copy from Torre del Greco, Italy, of a work Praxiteles considered one of his best. It is gentle, restrained, and at ease. The satyr is reclining against a pillar and serenely dousing himself with wine from a jar. The curve of the body is exaggerated. This style of sculpture heralded the Hellenistic period that began with the death of Alexander the Great in 323 B.C.

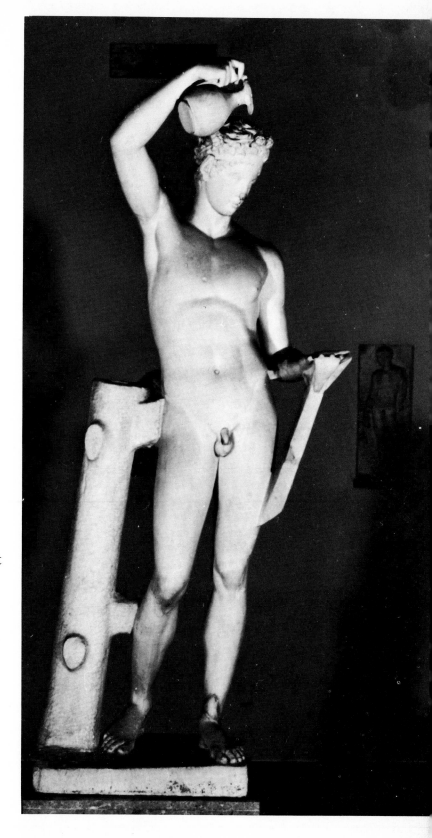

ROMAN. C. 220–230 A.D. *Dionysos, the Seasons, and Other Figures*
Marble sarcophagus, 35½ × 87¾ × 36¾ in.
The Metropolitan Museum of Art, New York
Joseph Pulitzer Bequest, 1955

Roman relief work very much in the Greek tradition. The carved
figures stand out boldly from the background. In the center is a
triumphant Dionysos seated on a panther with Pan just behind him. The
four large figures, two on each side, represent the four seasons. The
many joyful *putti* add immeasurably to the festive atmosphere of the
occasion.

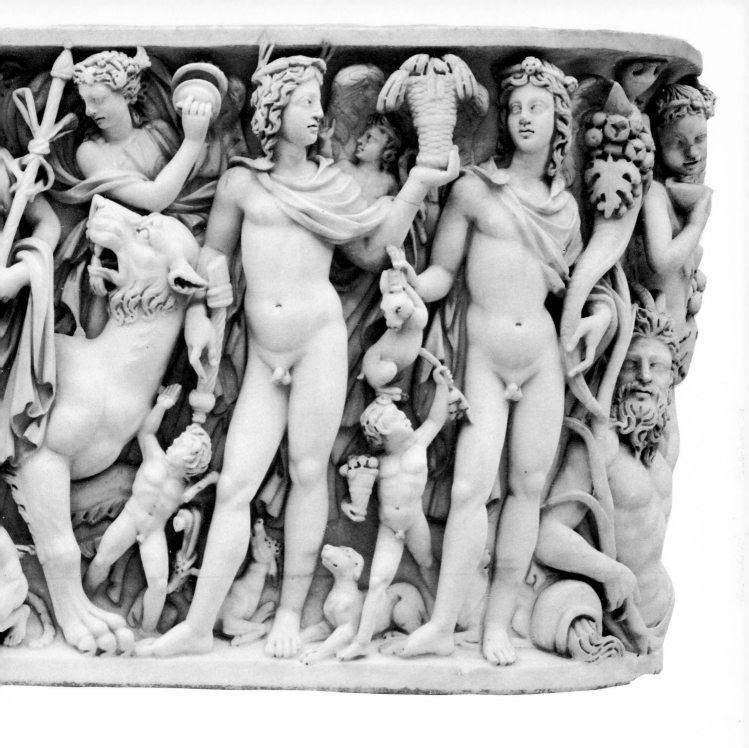

GREEK VASE PAINTING

Pottery-making is an ancient art having its origins in prehistoric times. From the beginning such ceramic ware was decorated according to the traditions of the periods. But it was left to the Greeks to adorn their wares with the finest form of storytelling and depiction of human figures, especially of the young male.

Toward the end of the seventh century B.C. the Athenians had become the leaders in the manufacture of ceramics, specifically in what is known as the period of black-figure vases, which lasted until about 530 B.C. In this technique solid black figures were painted on the natural red or yellowish color of the clay, and various details were then carved into the vase. The story was told in a single picture using large figures, and was at first usually based on Greek mythology having to do with the gods or on the Homeric legends. Soon scenes of secular life appeared, especially those of physical training, sports, and athletes in various poses. As in Greek sculpture, these were shown in the nude.

Around 530 B.C. a new process of vase painting developed, known as red-figure vase painting, which replaced the previous black-figure technique. The process was exactly reversed with the receptacle painted a black background while the figures were left in the original red color of the clay. For the next fifty years this technique was very popular, but then interest in vase painting virtually died out, although in southern Italy it lingered on until the third century B.C.

GREEK VASE PAINTING
Fifth century B.C.
Goddess and Youth
Red-figured bobbin, terra-cotta
Painted in polychrome on white ground
Attributed to the "Penthesileia painter"
*The Metropolitan Museum of Art
New York, Fletcher Fund, 1928*

More than one hundred vases have been attributed to this Greek painter renowned for his naturalistic style, and this work is considered one of his best. A Nike, moving gently forward, is crowning a victorious youth who is leaning backward. Since the Greek women were painted as if they were young males, there is a close similarity in features and form between the goddess and the nude youth.

GREEK VASE PAINTING
Fifth century B.C.
Red-figured krater
Young Athlete Preparing for a Prizefight
Staatliche Museen, Berlin

Since Greek athletic contests were always
fought in the nude there was danger, ever
present during the match, of tearing the
foreskin of the penis. Here a young
contestant is pulling his foreskin to the
front preparatory to tying it with a
narrow ribbon and thus preventing injury.

GREEK VASE PAINTING
Attic
Athletic Contest
Black-figured Panathenaic amphora
Museum of Fine Arts, Boston

37

38

opposite:

GREEK VASE PAINTING
South Italian
Maenad, Dionysos and Satyr
Red-figured column krater from Ruvo
Museum of Fine Arts, Boston

GREEK VASE PAINTING
South Italian
Three Young Warriors in Camp
Red-figured amphora
Frankfurt painter
Museum of Fine Arts, Boston

ROMAN
Second century A.D.
Portrait of a Boy
Portrait panel from a mummy
Encaustic on wood
*The Metropolitan Museum of Art
New York
Gift of Edward S. Harkness, 1917*

After the Romans conquered Egypt in
31 B.C. they modified the Egyptian
burial customs by substituting for the
usual bust an ornamented wooden board
with the portrait of the dead person. The
pigments used in these paintings were
mixed with hot wax. This young man
apparently died in his very early years.

opposite:
VITRUVIUS
(MARCUS VITRUVIUS POLLIO)
First century B.C.
Roman architect and engineer
*New York Public Library
Rare Book Division*

Vitruvius wrote and dedicated to Emperor
Augustus the standard work on
architecture called *De architectura libri X,*
which was to have a profound effect on
Michelangelo, Leonardo da Vinci, and
other Renaissance painters. In this
monumental work, Vitruvius propounded
his theories of drawing the human figure
according to geometric proportions and
illustrated his precepts with this drawing
of a young male encased in squares and
circles. Of course, the great artists of
the Renaissance expanded upon the
basics of Vitruvius and breathed their
own great genius into what they drew
and painted.

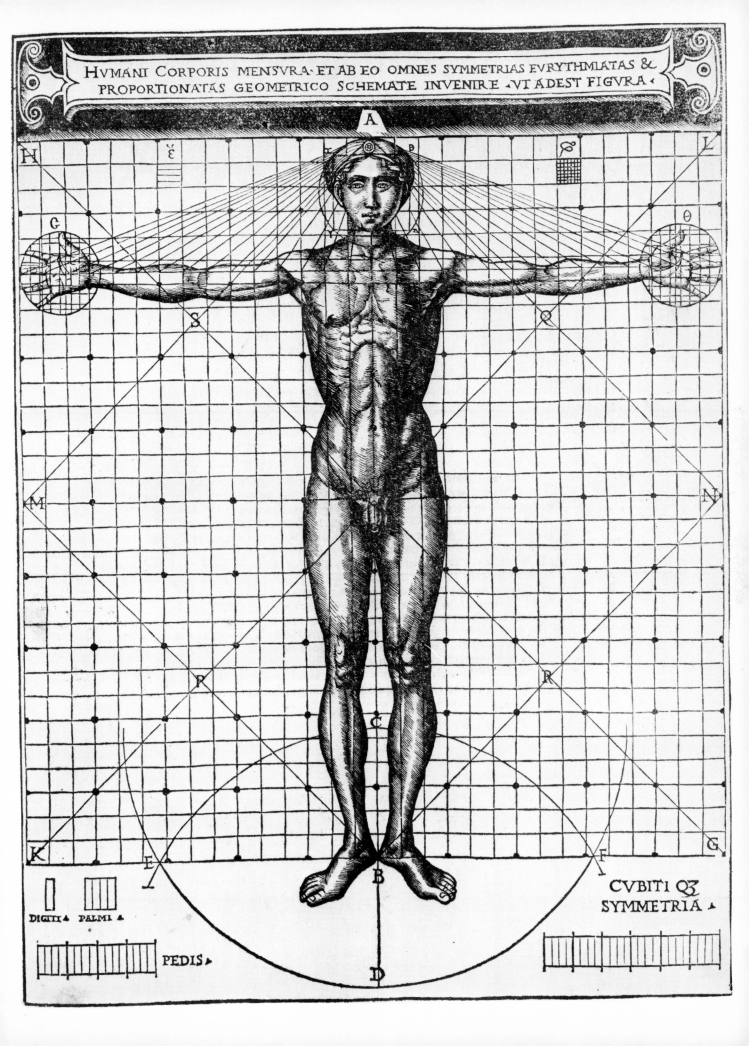

HVMANI CORPORIS MENSVRA·ET AB EO OMNES SYMMETRIAS EVRYTHMIATAS &
PROPORTIONATAS GEOMETRICO SCHEMATE INVENIRE ·VT ADEST FIGVRA·

DIGITI▲ PALMI▲

PEDIS▶

CVBITI Q3
SYMMETRIA ▲

MICHELANGELO BUONARROTI, 1475–1564, Italian
The Creation of Adam (detail), 1508–1512. *Sistine Chapel, Vatican, Rome*

This monumental figure of the creation of man is perhaps the most
famous part of the whole of Michelangelo's work on the ceiling of the
Sistine Chapel. The master of all Renaissance painters revived the
classical beauty of the Greek naked body but infused it with an intense
virile realism unknown to the Greeks and with the spirit of his own
deep religious faith. The finger reaching out to infuse life into the first
young man is that of God. Since this is long before Eden, the face of
Adam reflects only passive innocence, heightened by the soft contours of
his mouth.

PART II

During the Renaissance and Mannerist Periods

Inevitably the thousand years of the so-called Dark Ages, or the medieval years, came to an end, and the young male in art once again blossomed forth in all the beauty and glory that was his during the Golden Age in Greece. For hundreds of years the victorious Huns and Goths of the north had dominated the Western world, holding all in bondage in a feudal society, in which the arts had no chance to flourish except in the cold forbidding figures of well-draped saints that adorned their Gothic churches. Hidden away in the dustiest recesses of their dungeons and subject to hundreds of years of dirt and grime were the priceless classics of Greek literature, philosophy, and drama. Buried deep in the earth were hundreds of statues and paintings of the illustrious Greco-Roman civilization. For all these centuries art, at least in relation to the young male in art, was stagnant.

Then, about the beginning of the fourteenth century a faint stirring of portents of things to come took place. Scholars, especially Petrarch, began uncovering and discovering some of the hidden Greek classics. At once they became enamored of the Greek philosophy of beauty and freedom of individual behavior. And no wonder, after being cooped up so long by the repression of political feudalism and religious austerity. The pendulum had reached its apex and was slowly starting to come back. Early in the 1300s a painter named Giotto reacted against the stiff formality of medieval figures in art and began to endow them with features and forms closer to approximating living human beings. Because of this far-reaching and revolutionary innovation, Giotto is known as the father of the Renaissance, which was still almost a hundred years away.

During this hundred years many determining factors developed that made the flowering of the Renaissance possible. On the economic front around the year 1400 Italy was divided into a number of warring states engaged in commercial rivalry. Due to the massive growth of trade routes, both with the Western world and the East, a new class of wealthy merchants and bankers had sprung up. Because she was situated at the crossroads of world trade Italy, especially northern Italy, soon was enjoying a wealth so fabulous as to be beyond the imaginations of their Middle Age predecessors. Fabulous wealth brought competition, and thus the Italian states were constantly at war with one another. Wealth also brought luxurious living, a breakdown in the puritanical and ascetic concepts of religion, and an eagerness to acquire works of art, both for private collections and for public civic purposes. Foremost among the various Italian cities in the pursuit of artistic acquisition were Florence and Venice.

By now the scholars were assiduously ferreting out from musty vaults, studying, and interpreting the lost Greek and Roman classics. An era known as humanism was well under way, abetted by remarkable advancements in scientific knowlege and mathematical precepts. It was an era where attention was turned to the individual, his personal needs, and to the growing importance of the human body itself, as opposed to the dogmas of the established authority of the Middle Ages. Even the popes, their bishops, and the majority of the friars were as concerned in this period with the epicurean joys of the flesh as they were with the saving of souls. Political freedom was conducive to personal licentiousness, and were there not plenty of precedents in the newly unearthed pagan philosophies of the ancient Greeks? Emphasis on a future life was replaced by an avid interest in human and earthly concerns. Numerous archaeological finds were exciting patrons and artists alike. Such was the interest in these discoveries that Michelangelo unabashedly sold his first sculpture as a newfound original Roman piece. Pagan themes based on classical mythology became the order of the day and were most in demand by wealthy patrons.

Because Florence gave to the Renaissance its greatest artists and art patronage it can well be used to typify the role of the young male in art during this "rebirth of culture." Economically and politically Florence was dominated by the Medici family from 1428 when Cosimo became the ruling influence. The Medicis were rich bankers, who also owned a number of successful commercial enterprises. By lending vast sums of money to the state, by giving generously to civic enterprises, and by unstintingly patronizing the artists and writers, the millionaire Medicis were soon the sole ruling family in Florence, albeit not without envious enemies.

Such wealth, not only in Florence, but in all the Italian states as well as in Rome itself, had to be expended on good deeds as well as on warfare. So it was that the system of artistic patronage reached its highest point in art history during the Renaissance. The great patrons of the era were the popes in Rome who tried to outdo each other as they succeeded to the papacy in commissioning elaborate sculptural tombs and boldly conceived church paintings, the princes and aristocracy of the realms, and the rich industrialists. All vied for the services of the artists and encouraged any young talented hopefuls to become apprentices in the ubiquitous workshops of the master painters and sculptors.

In Florence under Cosimo de' Medici, until his death in 1464, many of the famous Renaissance artists flourished. Even before Cosimo, Florence had enjoyed the works of Nicola Pisano whose classic sculptures adorned the Baptistery of San Giovanni. Pisano's influence was strongly felt by Lorenzo Ghiberti, who spent innumerable years creating two sets of bronze doors for the Baptistery, the first started in 1401, the second in 1425. Like Pisano, Ghiberti was one of the first Renaissance artists to invoke the classic style and one of the early advocates of a new dimension in art, perspective. By the innovation of perspective, Renaissance art achieved a far greater realism than was known to the ancient Greeks.

This was the time of the Monumentalists, early Renaissance painters who added new realism and grandeur to their paintings and portrayed the young male with a new sensitivity.

They included Masaccio, Andrea del Castagno, Piero della Francesca, Mantegna, and Pietro Perugino, who was to exert a profound influence on Raphael. One Italian painter and engraver of this period, Luca Signorelli, took special interest in the male nude and his detailed physical makeup, with the result that he not only drew his figures in motion but combined an acute psychological insight into his human forms with an extremely accurate representation of their physical proportions.

To the revival of the classic style and the introduction of perspective, Donatello added another factor to the art of his day, a knowledge of anatomy. His *David,* a bronze done about 1430, was the first sculpture since the days of antiquity to be carved in the round. These and many other artists enjoyed Cosimo's patronage, including Fra Filippo Lippi, Veneziano, and Masaccio. As can be seen by the works of art that follow, all were concerned with the portrayal of the young male, often in the new vogue for portraiture but more frequently in the nude form of the classics.

For a short time after Cosimo's death his son Piero assumed charge of the Medici wealth, but being a sickly man, soon died. He was succeeded by his son Lorenzo the Magnificent, who held sway until 1492. If anything, these two accelerated the tempo of artistic patronage over what the generous Cosimo had contributed. Among their recipients was Antonio del Pollaiuolo, who was so concerned with anatomy that he dissected human corpses so that his drawings, especially *Battle of the Nudes,* could be authentic to life. Also concerned with anatomy was Andrea del Verrocchio, whose statue of *David,* done about 1465 for the Medici family, was the epitome to date of a bony structure with superb muscular detail and emotional expression. His was the last sculptural masterpiece of the early Renaissance. Also of this period was the epicurean painter Sandro Botticelli, whose simple purity and smoothness in portraying the natural human figure was soon to be replaced by the more psychological idealism of a new period of art called the High Renaissance.

Lorenzo's heirs were not competent to rule Florence, which soon became a Republic. But the ruling electorate was immediately dominated by a fanatically puritanical friar called Savonarola. While, like the later evangelists, he converted hundreds of Florentine citizens to his preachings of the renunciation of the pleasures of the flesh and the destruction of the pagan works of early Renaissance art, he soon embittered the ruling leaders in Florence and so angered Pope Alexander VI in Rome that he, along with two other friar compatriots, was hanged and his body burned to ashes. For a short time Savonarola's influence on art was immense. Both Botticelli and Michelangelo were disturbed and impressed by his attempts to reform the ways of the Church and to return it from its openly licentious living to its former moral plane. The struggle between Savonarola's quest for the good and chaste and the current state of the wickedness of man was to become visible in Michelangelo's unsurpassed paintings on the ceiling of the Sistine Chapel in Rome.

While the Republic in Florence continued with the help of the famous Machiavelli, in 1512 it was overthrown by the other Italian states when it persisted in allying itself with France, and once more the rule of the Medicis was restored. In 1513 Cardinal Giovanni de' Medici, son of Lorenzo, became pope as Leo X, and was followed by another Medici, Cardinal Giulio as Clement VII. Florence was now ruled from the papal chair, until 1531 when tyrant Alessandro de' Medici took over and ruled with brutal oppression.

During these turbulent years Florence could boast of having in its city the greatest artists of the High Renaissance, even the greatest of all times. While they did not stay in Florence, being called to Rome again and again by popes eager for their services, they were known as Florentine artists. Leonardo da Vinci went to Rome by way of Milan, Michelangelo by way of Bologna. Returning to Florence, Michelangelo from 1501 to 1504 created his magnificent eighteen-foot high nude statue of *David*, so entirely different from those of Donatello and Verrocchio.

Rome was seething with wealth, luxuriating in gold, silver, and bronze artistic creations, feasting, dancing, whoring, and collecting antiques and illuminated books. The statues and goldsmithing of Benvenuto Cellini were in great demand. Artists worked in many fields. Leonardo da Vinci invented amazing scientific instruments and designed ballet costumes, in addition to painting masterpieces. The sculptor Michelangelo became the world's greatest painter and a papal architect as well.

It is in the works of Michelangelo that the High Renaissance achieved a fame that has never been surpassed in art history. Michelangelo did not just copy the statues of the ancient Greeks. Like the Greeks he believed that "physical perfection is the mirror and emblem of a pure and noble spirit." So he carved and painted nudes, especially young male nudes, as the Greeks had done. But he endowed them with everyday reality combined with the spiritual turmoil of the High Renaissance period. A genius in anatomy and per-spective, he used these powerful techniques to depict the titanic struggle of tormented man caught between the good and evil forces of destiny, nowhere better illustrated than in his statue the *Dying Slave*. For Pope Julius II he spent four torturous years painting the story of the Creation on the Sistine Chapel ceiling and filling every nook and cranny with strong, muscular young male nudes. These decorative athletes, pictured in poses of superhuman contortions, powerfully convey the painter's psychological conviction that the human body and the human spirit are inseparable. Julius II died when Michelangelo was just thirty-eight and was succeeded by the youthful Leo X, who preferred the works of Raphael to those of either Leonardo da Vinci or Michelangelo.

By the end of the fifteenth century the influence of the Italian artists of the High Renaissance had begun to spread throughout the whole Western world, and no northern artist was more influenced by its trends than Albrecht Dürer in Germany. It was he who synthesized the then current medieval Germanic art with the new classicism of the Italian artists, with which he had first come in contact on a trip to Italy in 1494. He borrowed many of their classical themes, especially from the works of Pollaiuolo, and was especially impressed with their use of the first-century-B.C. Vitruvian man, whose rules of human proportion formed the mathematical bases for High Renaissance art. As in Italy, royal patronage was a boon to the arts of the north, and Dürer's patrons included Frederick the Wise and Emperor Maximilian.

There are many other Renaissance artists represented in this book, who used the young male to advantage in their works: from Italy, Jacopo de' Barbari, Bernardo Parentino, Il Sansovino, Vincenzo Danti; from the Netherlands, Hans Memling, Dirk Bouts; from

Germany, Bartholomäus Bruyn, Christoph Amberger, Ambrosius Holbein; from France, Pierre Dumonstier.

New schools of painting develop as a reaction against existing schools, and, true to form, Mannerism (about 1520–1600) superseded the High Renaissance in the latter half of the sixteenth century. The strict rules of the High Renaissance were too confining for the overwhelming emotionalism of some of the art masters, including Michelangelo, whose later fresco *The Last Judgment* was to influence so many with its manneristic exaggerations. Only by twisting and distorting the human figure could they achieve the rhythmic impact they wanted.

The word Mannerism was coined by Vasari to describe a diagrammatic painting based on imagination rather than on what the eye actually saw. The Mannerist artists did not haphazardly flout the stringent rules of the High Renaissance without knowing exactly what they were doing. They were striving for a subjective and emotional effect, a revolutionary art technique, just as on the religious and political front revoluntionary changes were taking place. A revolt within the Catholic Church was in progress, the outcome of which was the Reformation, or the breaking away of a large group of worshipers, the Protestants. Led by Martin Luther in Germany and Calvin in Switzerland, it was roundly denounced by Leo X, but he was ineffective in stopping its progress. In Germany the Diet of Augsbug in 1555 established the legality of Protestantism and split the Western world into two opposing religious camps. The effect of this schism upon the styles of art were to be monumental. For the moment, it was the unsettled factors which led to the Reformation that brought on a neurotic approach to painting by such artists as Pontormo, Parmigianino, El Greco, Benvenuto Cellini, and even Michelangelo himself. It was the great master's stress on the emotional presentation of the nude male body that so enormously influenced other artists and contributed to the Mannerist style. It lasted until the end of the sixteenth century, when it gave way to a return to naturalism embellished with decorative effects, a style known as Baroque. With the coming of the Baroque period, the influence of the Italian artists waned, and the opening of the seventeenth century saw the ascendancy in the arts of France, the Netherlands, and Spain.

GHIBERTI, LORENZO
1378–1455, Italian
Sacrifice of Isaac (detail)
C. 1401. Bronze
Museo Nazionale, Florence
Bertoni photo

As a young goldsmith of twenty-two, Ghiberti won a competition against seven leading sculptors of his day to execute the second pair of bronze doors for the Baptistery in Florence. One of the many scenes on the various panels was his interpretation of the biblical story of the *Sacrifice of Isaac.* Taking his inspiration from an Antique Greek torso, he fashioned this beautifully supple nude of the young Isaac.

DONATELLO (DONATO DI NICCOLÒ DI BETTO BARDI)
C. 1382–1466, Italian
David, c. 1430. Bronze, ht. 60⅛ in.
Museo Nazionale, Florence, Alinari photo

This Renaissance creation representing David is quite different from the David of Michelangelo that was to come some hundred years later. This portrayal is of a sensuous adolescent, effeminate, yet possessing strong physical energy, much in the style of Hellenistic sculpture, as contrasted with the works of Praxiteles or Myron. His triumphant smile and alluring body help make this one of the great masterpieces of Italian art.

49

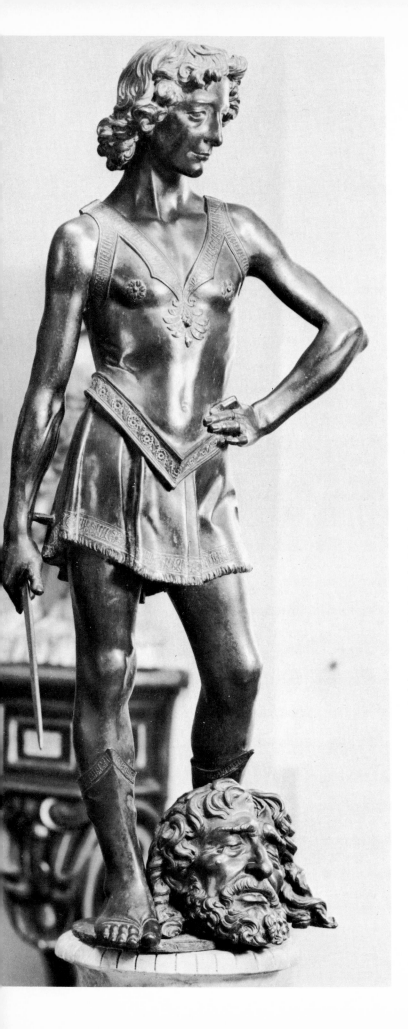

VERROCCHIO, ANDREA DEL
1435–1488, Italian
David, 1465. Bronze
Museo Nazionale, Florence, Bertoni photo

With Donatello's earlier *David* in mind,
Verrocchio added a great deal of effeminate
elegance to this statue, which was
originally done as a fountain figure. Here
we see almost a dandy, exuding ego and
youthful optimism, a sophisticated young
boy who is almost oblivious to his heroic
victory in slaying the giant Goliath. The
total effect is hardly that of monumental
proportions but rather of a delightfully
detached and handsome young victor.

PIERO DELLA FRANCESCA, 1410/20–1492, Italian. *Hercules*, c. 1460
Fresco in plaster, 59¼ × 49½ in.
Isabella Stewart Gardner Museum, Boston

Usually this artist painted only religious subjects. This pagan figure was
his one exception. With almost sculptural qualities, he has captured at
once the primitive simplicity of the Hercules legend and the massiveness
of his own art style. Painted for the Casa Graziani in San Sepolcro, it
was badly damaged when discovered in 1860 but has since been restored.

Here is the only surviving example of a master painter's work on a leather shield. Such decorated shields were used only for ceremonies, as leather would afford little protection in battles. It is one of the first examples of the early Renaissance drawing upon classical Greek art for inspiration. The young Greek athlete is reincarnated in the biblical David, shepherd king of Israel, who has just slain the giant Goliath, and who is beckoning on the Israelites to victory over the Philistines. The Florentines of this period loved the theme of the smaller conquering the larger as symbolic of their own struggles to remain free against powerful religious and secular outside forces.

MASTER OF THE ST. JOHN BUSTS
Italian. *Bust of St. John,* c. 1490
Terra-cotta, ht. 19½ in.,
with stand 25½ in.
Royal Ontario Museum, Toronto

The artist was so named by art critic Wilhelm von Bode because there are so many similar works apparently by the same person in museums both in America and abroad. Obviously a master of the High Renaissance, the Florentine artist worked beautifully in clay.

DOMENICO VENEZIANO
(DOMENICO DI BARTOLOMEO DI VENEZIA)
C. 1400–1462, Italian
Saint John in the Desert, 1445–1448. Panel, 11⅛ × 12¾ in.
National Gallery of Art, Washington, D.C.

According to Berenson, the artistic achievements of this artist consisted,
early in the Florentine Renaissance, of giving movement and expression
to the figure and an individuality to the face. This great work of art,
which influenced Domenico's followers for the rest of the fifteenth
century after his death, was one of fives scenes painted for the predella
of the S. Lucia dei Magnoli altarpiece in Florence.

opposite:
MANTEGNA, ANDREA, 1431–1506, Italian
David with the Head of Goliath. Canvas.
Kunsthistorisches Museum, Vienna

During the last years of his life, Mantegna produced some monochromes
on canvas, which he meant to resemble bas-reliefs and which he
painted against a marble background. It is another variation of the
Old Testament story. This David has a much more chunky and
muscular body than that of the lithe figure painted by Andrea del
Castagno on the leather shield.

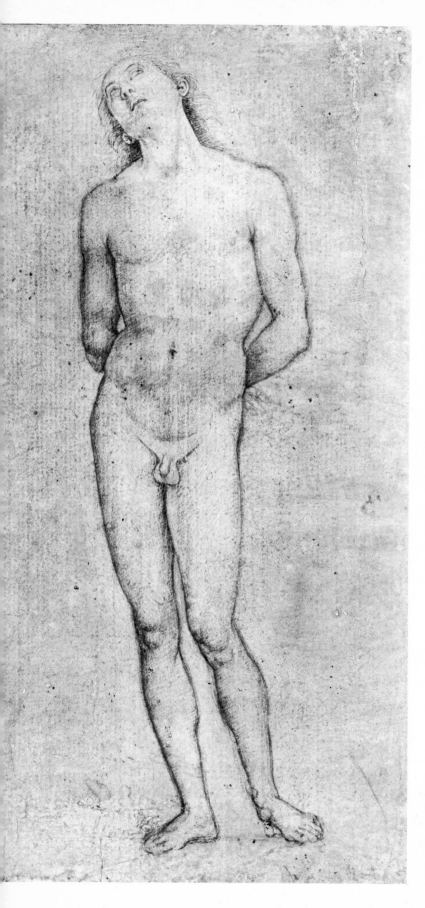

opposite:
PERUGINO
(PIETRO DI CRISTOFORO VANNUCCI)
C. 1450–1523
Italian. *Apollo and Marsyas*
Panel, 15⅜ × 11⅜ in.
Louvre Museum, Paris

Perugino had a truly sensitive feeling for the charm and beauty of young men. In this delicately executed interpretation of Greek mythology, he sets these classical figures in a romantic Umbrian valley with a Renaissance castle in the background overlooking a placidly moving stream. In a contest as to who played the sweetest music, Apollo won and, as his reward, tied Marsyas to a tree and beat him to death. But it is hard to imagine that this particular classical, Hellenistic Apollo, drawn with almost feminine grace and beauty, would do any such thing to such a gentle and pliant Marsyas.

PERUGINO
Saint Sebastian
Brush and brown ink over silverpoint
*The Cleveland Museum of Art,
Cleveland, Ohio
Dudley P. Allen Fund*

In contrast to the slimness of the Apollo in the painting, this drawing of the saint is thick-bodied and with even less muscular detail, all of which heightens the effectiveness of the pose.

56

MEMLING, HANS, C. 1435–1494, Flemish
Martyrdom of St. Sebastian, c. 1470
Musée Royale des Beaux-Arts, Brussels

Perhaps influenced by Rogier van der Weyden, Memling used everyday
figures and backgrounds, but enhanced them by his own spiritual
imagination. In this, another of the St. Sebastian legends, Memling's
own placid disposition reflects itself in the tranquil pose of this
rendition of the saint. He hardly seems to notice that four arrows have
already pierced his body. There is no heightened drama in this death;
even the archers seem as if engaged in target practice.

opposite:
LIPPI, FRA FILIPPO, C. 1406–1469, Italian. *Man and Horse*
Metalpoint drawing. *British Museum, London*

According to Vasari, "Fra Filippo drew exceedingly." Unfortunately
his existent drawings are very scarce, and it is more probable that this
one was not done by the master himself but in his studio by one of his
more talented apprentices.

POLLAIUOLO, ANTONIO DEL
(ANTONIO DI JACOPO D'ANTONIO BENCI), c. 1431–1498
Italian. *Battle of Naked Men,* c. 1470. Engraving, 15¾ × 23½ in.
Museum of Fine Arts, Boston

Here is undoubtedly one of the best-known drawings in the history
of art. It is also the first important copper engraving by an Italian artist
to show concern with the depiction of anatomy. According to Vasari,
this artist dissected many corpses in order to study their anatomy and
to find the muscles. The results show in this battle scene of straining
muscles and savage brutality. The whole scene is one of sadistic
fascination with the nude fighters full of tension and nervous fear.

opposite:
SIGNORELLI, LUCA, c. 1441–1523, Italian. *Two Figures Embracing*
Black chalk, 16 × 10⅜ in. *Louvre Museum, Paris*

With bold sweeping strokes the artist appears to have drawn these two
young men right out of life. Like other fifteenth-century artists he was
keenly concerned with anatomy. One nude is standing with his hands
on his hips; the other, his legs spread wide apart, has placed his arm
around the other's shoulders. There is obviously a certain psychological
and emotional attachment between the two. Some art critics consider
this drawing to be one of the finest studies of the male nude in
existence.

61

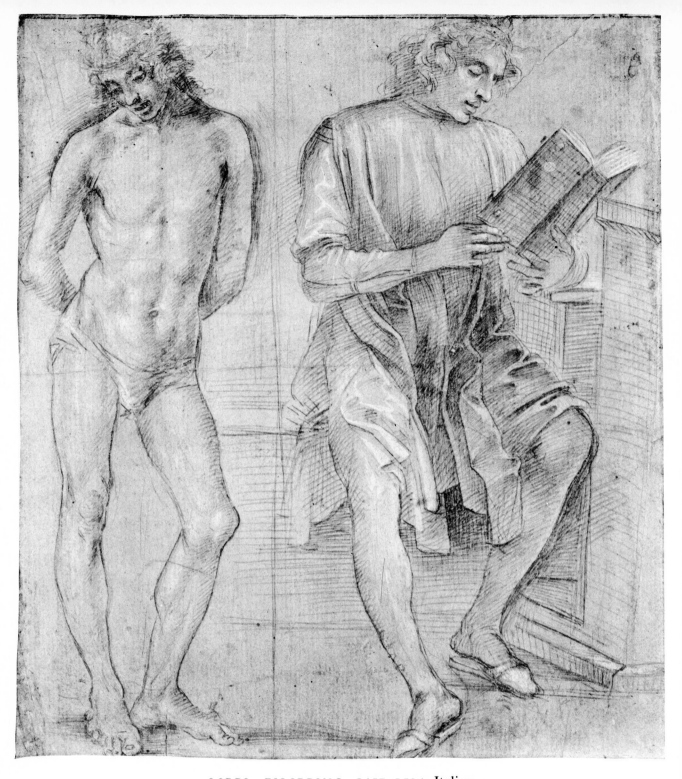

LIPPI, FILIPPINO, 1457–1504, Italian
Two Male Figures: Nude St. Sebastian and Seated Man Reading
Silverpoint and whitewash on pink paper, 9^{11}/$_{16}$ × 8½ in.
The Metropolitan Museum of Art, New York
Harris Brisbane Dick Fund, 1936

This artist worked in Florence in the studio of Botticelli, and the
seated young man reading the book is indicative of a usual studio pose
often drawn by Florentine artists. The nude St. Sebastian appears to be
a study for a painting with the figure possibly tied to a tree.

BARBARI, JACOPO DE'
C. 1450 or 1470–before 1516, Italian
Apollo and Diana
Drawing
National Gallery of Art, Washington, D.C.
Rosenwald Collection

This Venetian artist painted and drew according to the Renaissance-accepted Vitruvian formula of human proportions, that is, the central figure fits into geometrical circles and squares with the stance of the feet and the outstretched arm conforming to such limitations. Barbari drew very realistic figures. With Dürer, he often discussed these early Roman principles of the Vitruvian concept of man in art.

BOUTS, DIRK
C. 1410–1475, Flemish
Portrait of a Young Man, 1467
Silverpoint drawing on
gray-white prepared paper
5⁷/₁₆ × 4⁷/₃₂ in.
Smith College Museum of Art
Northampton, Massachusetts

This precise, lifelike drawing—possibly of another artist—may seem somewhat stiff, but it is delicately rendered and given a provincial Dutch dignity in the difficult media of silverpoint. It is somewhat in the style of another Dutch artist, Rogier van der Weyden, but much more minute in detail and bourgeois in subject matter.

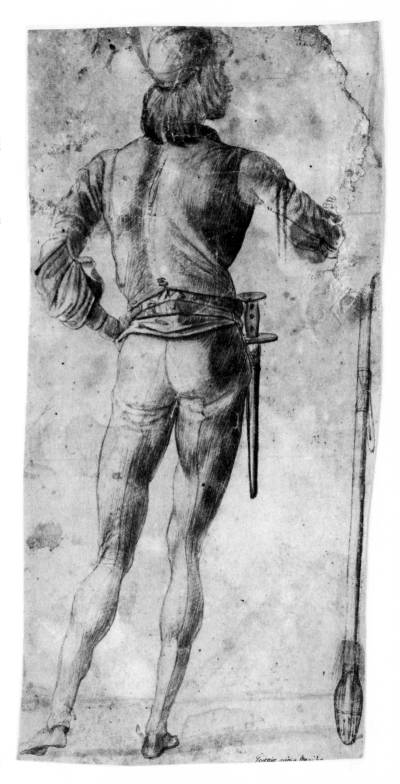

opposite:
PARENTINO, BERNARDO
1437–1531, Italian
Roman Prisoners and Trophies
Pen and bister drawing, 10⅜ × 8 in.
Christ Church, Oxford, England

This work somewhat obscures a clean delineation of the nude bodies of the prisoners by its emphasis on the cluttered weapons and other paraphernalia. It is clearly a forerunner of, but hardly in the same class with, the drawings of Pollaiuolo. This artist was an Augustinian monk from northern Italy, who rendered secular subjects, such as this drawing.

CARPACCIO, VITTORE
C. 1465–c. 1526, Italian
Young Man with Back Turned
Red and black crayon drawing with touches of wash
The Corcoran Gallery of Art
Washington, D.C.
William A. Clark Collection

A drawing that was originally attributed to the School of Ciorgione, but has now been reattributed to "after Carpaccio." It is an excellent example of a late Gothic costume, but it is quite simplified in order to show the contours of the body better. It is one of many drawings done as sketches for future paintings.

BOTTICELLI, SANDRO
(ALESSANDRO DI MARIANO FILIPEPI)
C. 1445–1510, Italian
St. Sebastian, 1474
Panel, 76¾ × 27¼ in.
Staatliche Museen, Berlin
Walter Steinkopf photo

According to Vasari, Botticelli was a
pupil of Fra Filippo Lippi, but he was
also influenced by Verrocchio and
Pollaiuolo. However, he possessed his
own particular style of rendering human
comeliness on canvas, whatever his
subject. This *St. Sebastian* was done for
the Church of S. Maria Maggiore,
Florence, and is noted for its refined and
erotic beauty.

opposite:
BOTTICELLI
Portrait of a Youth, c. 1476
Panel, 16 × 12 in.
National Gallery of Art, Washington, D.C.
Andrew Mellon Collection

Botticelli was a painter of the beauty of
both sexes. There is a great similarity
in the beauty of expression in his *Birth
of Venus* and in this portrait of a
Florentine youth, with his expressive
fingers, his long-flowing hair, and his
almost feminine mouth.

MASACCIO (TOMMASO CASSAI)
1401–1428, Italian
Profile Portrait of a Young Man, c. 1425
Panel, 16⅝ × 12¾ in.
National Gallery of Art, Washington, D.C.
Andrew Mellon Collection

This artist was one of the first of the
great painters of the Italian Renaissance
and probably did this portrait about the
same time he was working on his great
fresco *Sagra di Carmine.* It is somewhat
more severe than the others in this group.

LIPPI, FILIPPINO
1457–1504, Italian
Portrait of a Youth
Oil on panel, 20 × 13⅞ in.
National Gallery of Art, Washington, D.C.
Andrew Mellon Collection

Like so many of his contemporaries,
Lippi painted many portraits of young
males. This one is particularly expressive,
with the youth's studious and intelligent
expression made all the more striking by
the artist's use of a bare wall background
and the simplicity of the boy's attire.

68

BOLTRAFFIO, GIOVANNI ANTONIO
1466/67–1516, Italian
Portrait of a Youth
Panel, 18⁷/₁₆ × 13³/₄ in.
National Gallery of Art, Washington, D.C.
Ralph and Mary Booth Collection

Boltraffio, a pupil of Leonardo da Vinci, was completely influenced by him. He was noted for his classically beautiful faces, as seen in this young Milanese youth with his long-flowing tresses over his shoulders and his elegant costume.

PINTURICCHIO, BERNARDINO
C. 1454–1513, Italian
Portrait of a Youth, before 1490
Canvas, 20¹/₂ × 15¹/₈ in.
National Gallery of Art, Washington, D.C.
Samuel H. Kress Collection

An Umbrian youth of particularly refined splendor and aristocratic elegance is pictured before a romantically landscaped background. The artist has endowed this somewhat effeminate youth with the face of an angel.

BRONZINO, AGNOLO
(AGNOLO DI COSIMO DI MARIANO)
1503–1572, Italian
Ludovico Capponi
Oil on canvas
46 × 33¹⁵/₁₆ in.
The Frick Collection, New York

Influenced by Michelangelo and an
assistant to Pontormo, Bronzino was one
of the great Florentine Mannerist portrait
painters of his day. His portraits were
of sophisticated and aristocratic young
men, especially those of the Medici
family and their court. He presented
these youths in all their lavish elegance
of figure and dress.

BRONZINO

Portrait of a Young Man Writing
Museum of Fine Arts, Boston

70

BRONZINO
Portrait of the Grand Duke Francesco I dei Medici as Orpheus
Philadelphia Museum of Art, Philadelphia

In contrast to the elegant costumes in which Bronzino enveloped his subjects, here is a striking nude in the best Mannerist tradition with chiaroscuro highlights about the face and the thigh.

HOLBEIN, AMBROSIUS, 1494–c. 1519, German
Portrait of a Young Man
Oil on wood, 19¼ × 12¾ in. *Hermitage Museum, Leningrad*

The son of Hans Holbein the Elder studied with his illustrious father
and adopted his Renaissance style of painting. This is one of the best
in Ambrosius' short career.

AMBERGER, CHRISTOPH
C. 1500–1561/62, German
*Portrait of a Young Man in
Fur-Trimmed Clothes*
Oil on wood, 20 × 16¾ in.
Hermitage Museum, Leningrad

One of the most gifted painters of the
Augsburg school, Amberger's portraits
were of an aristocratic nature and done
in the realistic style of the German
Renaissance. The mood of this young
man is calm, and his features are
accurately portrayed. The fur-trimmed
clothes indicate that this subject was one
of the affluent citizens of the town.
While being enormously wealthy, they
nevertheless lived very modest private
lives, and Amberger painted them
accordingly.

BRUYN, BARTHOLOMÄUS, THE ELDER
1493–1555, German
Man with His Three Sons
1530. Oil on canvas
(transferred from wood), 10 × 18¼ in.
Hermitage Museum, Leningrad

One of the leading painters of the
Lower Rhenish region, Bruyn painted
the portraits of many of Cologne's most
illustrious citizens. Because he captured
with remarkable fidelity the personalities
of his subjects, his portraits are among
the finest of the sixteenth century. The
likeness of all three sons to their father
is superb, and the meaningful expression
of the son in the left corner of the
painting is especially endearing. The
picture is of a religious nature, therefore
the solemn tone.

DUMONSTIER, PIERRE
C. 1545–1610
French. *Portrait of a Youth*
Between 1550 and 1575
Oil on canvas, 12½ × 7½ in.
Hermitage Museum, Leningrad

This artist was one of the French sixteenth-century portraitists deeply interested in the psychology of his subject. The thoughtful expression, the set of the mouth, the anxious look in the wide-opened eyes show how deep the artist has penetrated into this boy's complex personality. Its intimate quality is enhanced by the close cropping of the head.

SARTO, ANDREA DEL
1486–1530, Italian
Portrait of a Sculptor
C. 1517. 28¼ × 22⅜ in.
National Gallery, London

There is wide speculation regarding this simple, frank, yet soulful, portrait. Some say it is of a sculptor holding a block of stone; others that he is a sensitive young man reading a book. Whichever, it remains a psychologically probing study of a young man evidently disturbed from his concentration by the viewer, and in his eyes is a flicker of momentary trepidation. The portrait is regarded as a masterpiece.

SALVIATI, FRANCESCO
1510–1563, Italian
Portrait of a Boy
50½ × 24 in.
National Gallery, London

Berenson at first ascribed this portrait to
Bronzino, but it has now become accepted
as being by Salviati. The youngster is
pictured full-length, dressed in an
elaborate red doublet over which he
wears a black, gold-embroidered coat.
His left hand clutches a sword handle.

opposite:
opposite:
MICHELANGELO BUONARROTI
1475–1564, Italian
David, 1501–1504
Marble, ht. 18 ft., ½ in.
Accademia Art Gallery, Florence

Here is the most famous statue in the
world, Michelangelo's High Renaissance
interpretation of a naked shepherd boy
with only a sling facing an armed-to-the-
teeth giant. It is a virile, heroic
masterpiece, quite unlike the more
effeminate Davids of Verrocchio and
Donatello. Here, inspired by the statues
of the Greeks of the Golden Age,
Michelangelo embodies all that is good
and beautiful in a youth ready to fight to
victory over all the evil forces in this
world. Regarding the statue itself,
Michelangelo has added outlines of ribs
and a semblance of muscles to the
smoothness and idealism of the nude
bodies of Greek sculpture, thus
achieving a reality which did not concern
the Greeks. No pagan God, this David,
but a very human hero, yet breathless in
its sheer beauty and forcefulness.

MICHELANGELO
Dying Slave
1513–1516
Marble, ht. 8 ft., 6½ in.
Louvre Museum, Paris

In this voluptuous work, Michelangelo
embodies pathos and resignation. It
almost appears as if, rather than dying,
the young captive has fallen asleep. Yet
he is aware that he is soon to leave this
world. With a sensual weariness and a
fleeting feeling of loss as to the joys he
might have experienced in life had his
lot been different, he serenely submits to
his fate.

76

opposite:
MICHELANGELO
Seated Nude
1508–1512
Sistine Chapel, Vatican, Rome

In discussing the works of Michelangelo, Berenson remarked that "there was [for him] no other such instrument for conveying material significance as the human nude." He felt that no other artist ever surpassed Michelangelo in stimulating our imagination and arousing our senses by the sheer beauty and forcefulness of his nudes. This nude masculine young man bears a close resemblance in body and features to Adam.

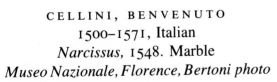

CELLINI, BENVENUTO
1500–1571, Italian
Narcissus, 1548. Marble
Museo Nazionale, Florence, Bertoni photo

Primarily a goldsmith, Cellini brought a jeweler's love of detail, often irrelevant, to his sculptures. To the Mannerism of his day he added new twists and extensions of the classical figure. Thus, this handsome youth, in love with himself, sits in an unnaturally twisted pose with his arm swung uncomfortably over his head. The legs, too, assume a difficult two-level stance. However, the full effect of this mythological youth is electrifying.

ITALIAN
Sixteenth century
Mercury. Bronze
National Gallery of Art, Washington, D.C.
Andrew Mellon Collection

A beautifully formed body of a Greek
god in the best Mannerist tradition, this
statue has a close affinity to two Davids:
Donatello's and Michelangelo's. Both in
the sculptured contours and in the relaxed
pose with his lower legs crossed, this
work is very human and natural, as if
Mercury had just stepped out of real
life.

opposite:
SANSOVINO, IL (JACOPO TATTI)
1486–1570, Italian
Bacchus, 1510. Marble
Museo Nazionale, Florence

Like Raphael, Sansovino could carve a
piece of unequaled sensuous beauty. His
works stand on a par with Michelangelo.
But this *Bacchus* is not a Greek or
Roman god; he is typically Tuscan. The
body is soft and sensuous, the expression
one of anticipated pleasure at the thought
of drinking the wine, not the drunken,
orgiastic pose usually ascribed to this
god. This nude youth radiates adolescent
enchantment. It is probable that a young
studio assistant of the sculptor posed as
his model for this Florentine masterpiece.

SANSOVINO
St. John. Wood, ht. 25½ in.
Fogg Art Museum, Harvard University
Cambridge, Massachusetts
Grenville L. Winthrop Bequest

This statue is thought to be of the
youthful St. John, but is in question,
both as to its subject and its attribution
to Sansovino.

DANTI, VINCENZO
1530–1576, Italian
Honor Triumphant over Falsehood
Marble
Museo Nazionale, Florence, Bertoni photo

Done not too many years after
Michelangelo's *Slaves*, this is an excellent
example of Renaissance sculpture in the
Mannerist style. Here is tremendous
energy in action as the hand of Honor
is in the act of pulling out the tongue
of Falsehood.

opposite:
PARMIGIANINO
(FRANCESCO MAZZOLA)
1503–1541, Italian
Cupid Carving His Bow
1530. Oil on panel, 53¼ × 25½ in.
Kunsthistorisches Museen, Vienna

A painter from northern Italy,
Parmigianino was a leader in the
Mannerist school of art, who insisted
his paintings create a pleasurable
sensation. This figure of Cupid has been
accepted as a deliberate homosexual
rendition. The artist, who himself had a
beautiful body and the face of an angel,
could very well have used his own image
in a mirror as a model. He has
exaggerated the boy's body around the
buttocks and in the softness of the flesh.
The expression in Amor's eyes is sly
and maliciously inviting of physical
contact. The nude body is posed with
the left foot standing triumphantly on
two books, symbolizing the victory of
physical love over science and
knowledge.

83

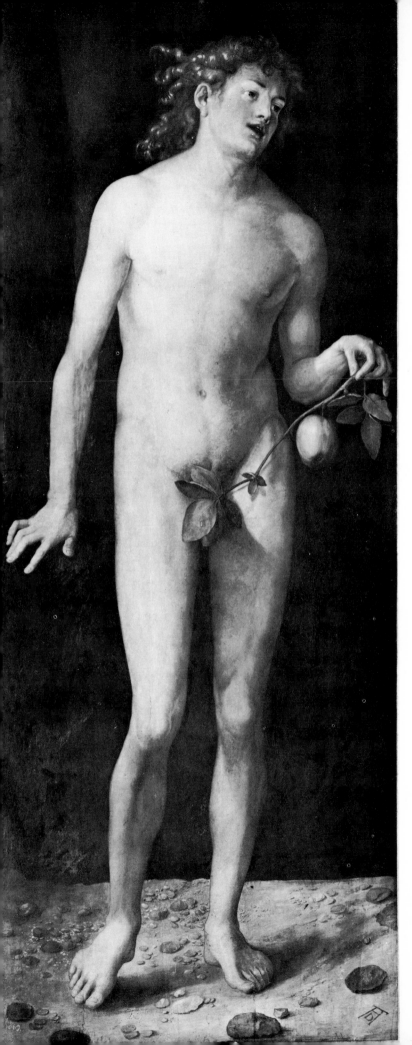

DÜRER, ALBRECHT
1471–1528, German
Adam, 1507
Panel, 82¼ × 31⅞ in.
Prado Museum, Madrid

This is one of two panels. The other is of Eve. While Dürer intended to paint this young Adam as the perfect classical human form, he endowed the smooth figure with few anatomical proportions. The result is a lyrical, anticlassical young male appearing quite feminine, with his long and disarrayed locks of hair and the affected manner in which he holds the tree branch between his thumb and index finger. The body appears to be swaying, not firm. This *Adam* is in complete contrast to Michelangelo's virile, though sensitive, *Creation of Adam.*

opposite top:
DÜRER
Self-Portrait at the Age of Thirteen
1484. Silverpoint drawing
Albertina Museum, Vienna

Here is the earliest drawing in existence by Dürer. It was done while beginning his art studies in Nuremberg. By looking in the mirror and sketching himself, the young artist created this masterful rendition in the style of the late Gothic period, but with an unusual delicacy of his own as yet undeveloped style.

DÜRER
Arion, c. 1514
Brush drawing and watercolor with
contours in pen
Kunsthistorisches Museen, Vienna

This is a mythical classical episode of
the seventh century B.C. in which the
poet Arion is being rescued from the sea
by a huge dolphin. The poet clutches his
precious lyre with his left arm as his
naked body straddles his rescuer whose
head he grasps with his right arm. Dürer
on his visit to Italy in 1495 had become
enamored of the classical beauty of the
human form he found in the Italian
Renaissance works and drew many
sketches of myths and allegories full of
the spirit of Greek antiquity.

PISCE SVPER CVRVO VECTVS CANTABAT ARION

RAPHAEL (RAFFAELLO SANTI), 1483–1520, Italian
Nude Male in Action. Drawing. *Szépmüvészeti Museum, Budapest*

One of the chief exponents of the classical art of the High Renaissance,
this artist worked to re-create the glory of ancient Rome.

CHIMENTI, JACOPO (JACOPO DA EMPOLI), c. 1554–1640, Italian
Young Man Seen from the Back. Red chalk, stumped, 16 × 10⅟₁₆ in.
The Pierpont Morgan Library, New York

A partial nude can be as sensuous as a complete nude. This young
man, stripped to the waist, possesses a strong muscular back, which the
artist has highlighted with bold, flowing strokes, while rendering the
folds of the lower clothing in minute detail.

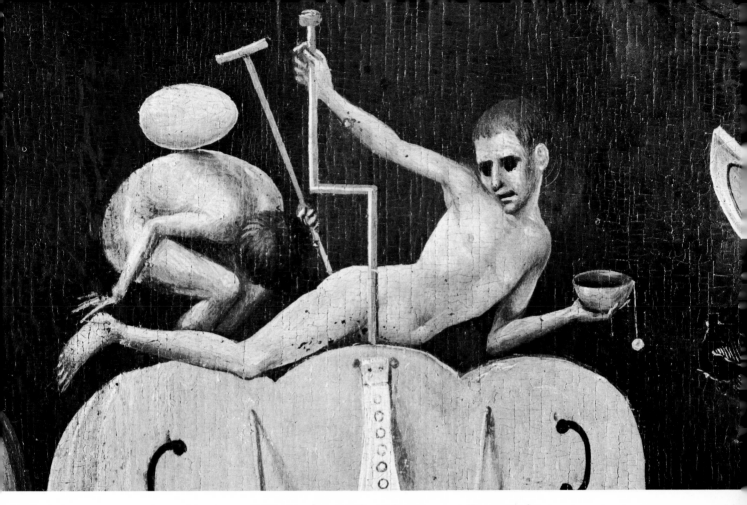

BOSCH, JEROME (HIERONYMUS VAN AEKEN)
C. 1450–1515?, Flemish
The Garden of Earthly Delights (detail). *Prado Museum, Madrid*

Bosch is probably the most enigmatic painter of all times. The weird and fantastic figures he painted were very much concerned with Protestant fundamentalist beliefs in sin, hell, and eternal damnation. Thus, what he shows in his *The Garden of Earthly Delights* is just the sort of earthly behavior that will send these already lost souls to the consuming flames in the hereafter. It is peopled with numerous grotesque figures engaged in sensuous and licentious pleasures.

opposite:
PONTORMO (JACOPO CARUCCI), 1494–1556/57, Italian
Nude Boy Seated, c. 1520
Red chalk, 16 × 10¼ in. *Uffizi Gallery, Florence*
Alinari-Art Reference Bureau photo

A devout follower of the style of Michelangelo, Pontormo was considerably more refined in his sketches, but equally as well known in his day for his drawings as the master himself and as Leonardo da Vinci. The boy's body is thrown back, his legs wide apart, and he is pointing at something with his right arm, evidently with great agitation. This is possibly a study, which was never used, for the artist's lunette in the Medici villa at Poggio a Caiano.

NORTHERN ITALIAN
Fifteenth century
Young Man with a Lance. Drawing
The Pierpont Morgan Library, New York

Another Renaissance drawing by an
unknown artist delightfully illustrating
the costume of the day. Undoubtedly
this was a study for a detail of a large
painting.

opposite:
GRECO, EL (DOMENIKOS THEOTOKOPOULOS)
C. 1541–1614, Greek-Spanish. *St. Martin and the Beggar*
C. 1597. Canvas, 76⅛ × 40½ in.
National Gallery of Art, Washington, D.C., Widener Collection

El Greco came to Spain from Crete after studying in Venice. He
settled in Toledo. Between 1597 and 1599 he painted three retables for
the Chapel of S. José, all done in his newly developed style of distorted
figures and twisted backgrounds. In this painting each of the two figures
stretches a long way up from the bottom and a long way down from the
top of the canvas respectively. Both the nude beggar and the armored
saint are extremely youthful in form and facial expressions.

91

CARAVAGGIO. *Amor Victorious* or *Eros Triumphant*, c. 1600
Staatliche Museen, Berlin, Walter Steinkopf photo

This bold projection of a victorious youth, the model for which was
picked up off of the streets by Caravaggio, has best been described by
Bernard Berenson: "I clearly see a youthful nude, well-proportioned,
firm-fleshed, fine-limbed in a diagonal pose. He is amused. It will be
such a lark to see these silly human bipeds hit by his darts, and going
mad with the sweet poison."

PART III

In the Seventeenth and Eighteenth Centuries

Like all historical, political, and religious movements, periods of changes in art do not always fit into the neat categories of centuries or part centuries. It would be easy to say that Mannerist art went out with the sixteenth century and Baroque art entered with the beginning of the seventeenth century. But that would be reckoning without an Italian painter, who today stands in the ranks of Leonardo da Vinci, Michelangelo, and Raphael, a painter whose naturalism and realism revolutionized art for hundreds of years—namely, Michelangelo Caravaggio. This short-lived youthful painter from a place near Milan came to Rome an unknown, only to become a celebrity almost overnight, all because he introduced a revolutionary new style of painting and subject matter. First, he painted exactly what he saw, ugly or beautiful; second, his subjects were painted as real as the everyday people of the streets he used as models; and third, he exposed the nude bodies of enticing boys and young males in his own special chiaroscuro style that left the art patrons of Italy gasping.

Two other Italian painters of influence during this period failed to fit into the Baroque category: Annibale Carracci and his cousin Lodovico. They were the leaders of an eclectic school of art, whose followers tried to assimilate the best of the High Renaissance and other Renaissance styles. In this they were encouraged by the newly founded Jesuits, a product of the Counter-Reformation in the Catholic Church, in which the licentious freedom of the clergy was replaced by the austere monastic life of the medieval church. They urged Catholic painters to dramatize Church doctrines in order to help bring back wavering church members into the fold, and to be extremely literal in their paintings on the subject of miracles.

It was this new religious force that was the vital element in soon developing a full-fledged Baroque style in art that swept from Italy to the northern countries and to France and Spain. Perhaps the artist most responsible was Gian Lorenzo Bernini, in his day the most prominent artist in all of Italy. It was his style of portrayal of religious exaltation and mystic rapture, intensified with excitement and movement, that set the stage for Baroque artists all over Europe.

From Flanders to Rome in 1600 came a twenty-three-year-old Flemish artist, Peter Paul Rubens, who was immediately attracted to the works of Carracci and Caravaggio and developed this interest into a flourishing Baroque style all his own, peopled with sensuous, fleshy female nudes. Catholic Flanders was impressed with his Baroque religious and allegorical subjects and the dramatic and emotional theatricalism he brought to them.

In neighboring Protestant Holland, however, such Baroque style had little effect. Composed of a society of rich merchants and a hard-working middle class with a somewhat English-Puritan outlook, art buyers preferred genre subjects showing everyday life in the home, roistering in the taverns, or kitchen tables bursting with food and drink. No papal courts or tyrannical princes to act as art patrons, the well-to-do Dutch people themselves were the art patrons. Thus the nudes of Rome and Flanders gave way to dignified and realistic portraits of such leading citizens as aldermen and burgomasters. Onto this scene came the leading painter and draftsman of all time in the Protestant north, Rembrandt van Rijn. Like other Dutch artists his specialty was portraits, of which he did so many of himself at various stages of his life that they constitute a pictorial autobiography. He did not stop at portraits, but in a style completely individual to himself, he painted innumerable other subjects, religious and human scenes and experiences, all rendered with faithful reality and a stress on human significance and with a chiaroscuro derived from Caravaggio but individualized by himself.

Baroque art spread to Spain and was most evident starting with the later works of El Greco and progressing to those of Francisco de Zurbarán and Diego Velázquez. While a third Spanish painter, Jusepe de Ribera, was doing nude male figures in the manner of Caravaggio, these other two were furthering the cause of the Baroque style along two other lines. Zurbarán was known for his monastic works, while Velázquez, as court painter to Philip IV, transformed the stiff and rigid portraits of the Renaissance periods into vital, living, albeit aristocratic, people. At the same time, on the other side of the street, so to speak, Spain's most popular painter, Bartolomé Esteban Murillo, was painting the daily life and street scenes of the people of Seville. He was particularly loved by the Spanish people for his sentimental portrayals of street urchins and endearing youngsters eating fruit. Late in the eighteenth century saw Goya both as the official court painter and a painter of young boys, as well as being known for his biting satirical works.

But it was in France under the rule of a paternal and authoritative monarch, Louis XIV, that Baroque art reached its zenith during the long period of peace in Europe. The two men most responsible for finally bringing about this situation, and thus laying the foundation for the long rule of Louis XIV, were Cardinal Richelieu, who dominated France from 1624 to 1642, and his successor, Mazarin, who effected two important treaties: the Treaty of Westphalia in 1648 with the Holy Roman Empire and the Treaty of the Pyrenees in 1659 between France and Spain. When Louis, on the death of Mazarin, finally took over the reins of government in 1661, he was to enjoy many peaceful years until his death in 1715, years in which the court life of an absolute monarch shaped the Baroque style of art in France. The classical rules of Rome prevailed in this art, but now, reflecting the elegance of the court, much decorative detail was added, thus designating it as Baroque. The greatest symbol of this style, however, was in architecture, not in painting, in the form of the most fabulous Baroque edifice ever built, Louis XIV's Palace of Versailles, constructed between 1660 and 1680. In painting two great artists led the rest, Nicolas Poussin and later Charles

Le Brun, neither of whom concerned himself much with the young male in art. As the seventeenth century ended and the eighteenth began, the most accepted French painter was Jean-Antoine Watteau, whose works formed a transition from the Baroque to a new embellishment of Baroque, known as Rococo.

Louis XIV finally died after one of the longest reigns in history, too long. The aristocracy of the French court, held in hand by a classically minded autocratic monarch, were chafing at the bit to let go and enjoy their individual freedoms outside of the activities that almost totally centered on court life. Louis's grandson came to the throne as Louis XV and turned out to be a godsend for the aspirations of the aristocracy, for Louis himself craved the privacy of his own apartments to the pomp and circumstance of court functions. While court was in session he remained the absolute monarch, but at all other times he would repair to his own quarters and enjoy the informality of a private citizen. Thus French society was at last free to entertain lavishly in their own mansions, making court appearances only when necessary. It naturally followed that if their mansions were to be the scenes of their frivolous revelries they must be furnished and decorated in the most elaborate manner possible, yet whimsically enough to reflect the shallow personality of the whole confectionary charade. It is in this setting that Rococo art flourished.

The pursuit of youthful love and the passionate flirtations were the mainstays of this Rococo age. Wealthy beyond imagination, the sole purpose of living for these French aristocrats was the quest for pleasure. They abandoned themselves to the bacchanalian delights of the moment, and in this they invited the rich middle class to join. Never before had the hard core of aristocracy been so penetrated. Even the king took a commoner, Madame de Pompadour, as his mistress, and put her in charge of decorating his many establishments. The paintings, sculptures, and much assorted bric-a-brac that filled these homes to overflowing were the decorative accessories to this age of unblighted love. It was an era in which beautiful women were worshiped, and the nude female figure almost obliterated the young male in art. But not quite. The sculptures of Clodion were in constant demand because they consisted mostly of erotic nude statuettes of bacchantes and fauns that satisfied the sensual cravings of the period. These were frivolous renderings of the classics, embellished with ornate decorations, perfect examples of the day's salon and boudoir art.

Another sculptor whose works titillated their wealthy buyers was Antoine Denis Chaudet. His statues began in the best of the Roman classical style but soon took on a saccharine sentimentality that immediately endeared them to fashionable French society. On the other hand, one painter did emerge in this period who was really not of it, Jean-Baptiste-Siméon Chardin. Not all the middle class in France could join or even wanted to emulate the cream of society, and their interests in art were far from the extremes of Rococo. To this group appealed the dignity and simplicity of Chardin's works, a welcome relief from the overfastidiousness of court paintings and sculptures.

Another so-called renegade from Rococo was Jean-Baptiste Greuze who was perhaps more revered in the czarist courts of Russia than in his own country. He painted his portraits more in the Dutch style than with the pompous pretentiousness of the prevailing French manner.

At first blush it would seem that the eighteenth century in France was one of the freest in history, having released itself from the shackles of the past, yet, as history records, it was filled with the seeds of its own destruction. While the rest of the world strove mightily to emulate the Court of France and its lascivious aristocracy, the suffering masses of the people of this French nation, hungry from want of bread, let alone cake, formed a fertile breeding ground for the coming revolution. It was the French Revolution that put an abrupt end to all Rococo art. The paintings and sculptures so enjoyed by the aristocracy were not for the people of the Revolution. Those artists who had begun creating in the Rococo style immediately turned to the more rigid style of the classics and to subjects glorifying the Revolution. Jacques-Louis David, who as a Deputy of the People had voted in 1793 for the death penalty for Louis XIV, became "Dictator of the Arts" for the proletariat, and the age of Neoclassicism in art was born.

Before the eighteenth century, England had very little art of its own, relying instead on the works of imported artists such as Anthony van Dyck. Now an age of reason prevailed in which the leading art form was the portrait, and to a lesser extent landscape paintings. These portraits were refined and full of the social graces, in fact they were known as society portraiture. As in France, the subjects for most of these portraits were members of the royal and aristocratic families. Thomas Gainsborough was the leading painter in this field. He is probably best known for his *Blue Boy*. It was in this typical manner that the young male was presented in English art of the eighteenth century. There was in this period almost a complete absence of the nude in both paintings and sculpture. These were to come in the next century when William Etty daringly introduced the classic male nude to an astonished English audience. However, mention must be made of an engraver named William Blake, thought mad by his late eighteenth-century contemporaries, who did draw nude young males in fantastic classical forms of his own imagination. But it was almost a century later before his rightful place in English art was recognized.

CARAVAGGIO, MICHELANGELO MERISI DA

1573–1610, Italian

No painter in history captured the young male in art as did Caravaggio, nor exerted more influence on succeeding artists in their renderings of young males. He was the exponent of the chiaroscuro style, in which he highlighted the nude bodies and resplendent faces of his young men against shadowy backgrounds. Bellori, according to Berenson, characterized Caravaggio the man as brilliant, inspiring, attractive; on the other hand he was quick-tempered, intolerant, quarrelsome, and (perhaps) a homosexual. Berenson, for his part, was more concerned with Caravaggio as an artist and ends his essay on this painter: "For me he is perhaps the most serious as well as the most interesting painter that Italy produced between Tintoretto and Tiepolo." In his own time, when Rome was exalting the religious beauty and nobility of the Virgin and the saints, Caravaggio was not held in quite such esteem, but was taken to task for his use of gross and earthy models, his vulgarity, and his unorthodox paintings. Today Caravaggio in his own way is considered a master along with Michelangelo, whose influence on him was profound.

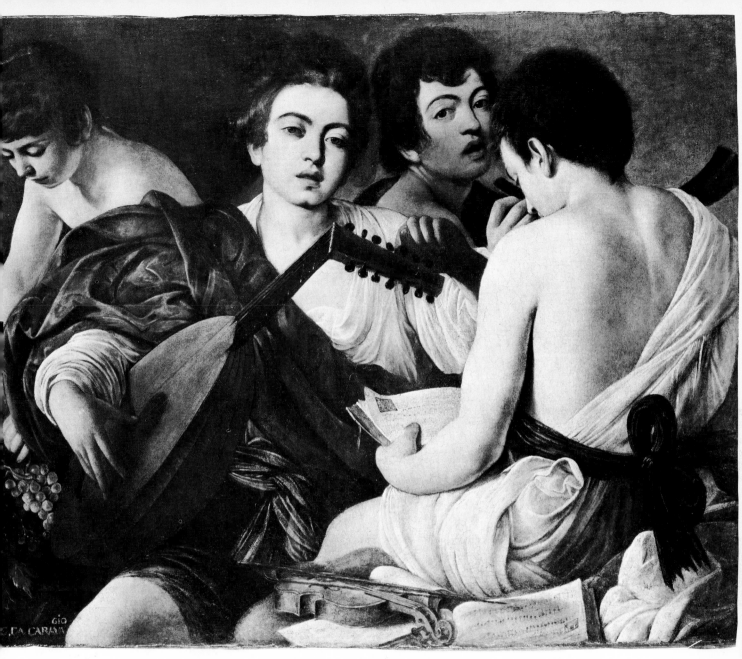

CARAVAGGIO. *The Musicians*. Oil on canvas, 36¼ × 46⅝ in.
The Metropolitan Museum of Art, New York, Rogers Fund, 1952

Caravaggio often used the same boy as his model in several of his
works; for example, the boy at the left peeling fruit also appears in his
painting, *Boy Peeling Fruit*. He was also very fond of using musical
instruments as similar background material in various paintings, and
those used here are also to be seen in *Amor Victorious*. He painted
these four cherub-faced handsome youths, who blend so harmoniously
together, for Cardinal del Monti. The parted lips of the two boys in the
middle add to the extreme sensuousness of the scene.

GALLIADI COPY AFTER CARAVAGGIO. *The Card Players*
Fogg Art Museum, Harvard University, Cambridge, Massachusetts
Gift of Dr. Lloyd Cabot Briggs

opposite:
CARAVAGGIO. *St. John the Baptist*, c. 1602–1604
Oil on canvas, 68¼ × 52 in.
William Rockhill Nelson Gallery of Art, Kansas City, Missouri
Nelson Fund

Caravaggio always needed a model before him and always copied nature
true to life. He was a past master in selecting young males that exuded
sexuality and conveying their full-flowing sensuousness to canvas. Here
is a sitting and brooding St. John, his glimmering, beautiful body
strikingly emerging from a shadowy background.

CARRACCI, LODOVICO, 1555–1619, Italian. *Nude Sleeping Boy*
Red chalk drawing on paper originally cream-colored, 9⁵/₁₆ × 8⁷/₈ in.
Ashmolean Museum, Oxford, England

As head of the Carracci Academy in Bologna, this artist stressed to
his pupils that they should closely study nature and that they should pay
particular attention to the nude. Thus, this anti-Mannerism and
exceedingly realistic drawing of an unclothed sleeping boy in a
completely relaxed, if somewhat difficult, position, legs apart, and with
a happy smile of contentment on his cherubic face.

opposite:
CARACCIOLO, GIOVANNI BATTISTA (BATTISTELLO),
1570–1637, Italian. *St. Sebastian.* Oil, 80 × 45 in.
*Fogg Art Museum, Harvard University, Cambridge, Massachusetts
Gift of Herbert and Arthur Pope, Edward W. Forbes, and Paul J. Sachs*

This Neopolitan painter was obviously influenced by Caravaggio's
chiaroscuro technique. The emphasis is on the entire body of the saint,
but what is most striking is that the partially opened mouth, expressing
both pain and pious resignation, gives an earthy, sensual appeal.

101

GUERCINO
(BARBIERI, GIOVANNI FRANCESCO)
1591–1666, Italian
Standing Boy Holding a Bowl
Red chalk, 10⁷/₁₆ × 7⁷/₁₆ in.
The Metropolitan Museum of Art
New York, Rogers Fund, 1963

As a young artist Guercino was introduced
to the Carracci brothers and adopted
some of their drawing techniques. His
work with red chalk was bolder but less
polished than his many later drawings in
pen and ink. This study might be a
sketch of Ganymede, the cupbearer to
the gods, but it was never used in any
of his known finished paintings.

opposite:
BERNINI, GIAN LORENZO
1598–1680, Italian
Naked Youth Sitting
Drawing, red chalk heightened in white
Staatliche Graphische Sammlung, Munich

This could well be a self-portrait done
by Bernini as a young man, for he was
known to use a mirror and draw his own
features and emotions. This seated naked
boy with a strong physique is evidently,
by the expression on his face and his
open mouth, awed at something unknown
to the viewer.

ITALIAN. Unknown draftsman of the seventeenth century
Male Nude. Charcoal on greenish paper
Staatliche Graphische Sammlung, Munich

This anonymous artist was a master at drawing the human physique in action as seen in this dramatic stance with the left knee resting on a block.

CECCO BRAVO (FRANCESCO MONTELATICI)
1607–1661, Italian. *Youthful St. John the Baptist*
Red chalk with traces of white chalk, 15¾ × 10 in.
Janos Scholz Collection, New York

This Florentine artist was a devotee of Andrea del Sarto, and his works reflect this influence. Cecco Bravo did a series of nude male drawings of which this is one of the most remarkable. St. John was a particular favorite of his, and he drew him in many and various poses.

105

PRETI, MATTIA, 1613–1699, Italian
The Young Bacchus. 37³/₈ × 50¹/₂ in.
Städelschen Kunstinstituts, Frankfurt, Germany

Obviously a follower of Caravaggio, Preti added his own original style
and immense vigor to his painting. He was one of the originators of
the grand decorative period of Neopolitan painting. Thus, in this nude
figure of Bacchus pulling on stems of lush, ripe grapes, he has
exaggerated the proportions of the figure itself and the prominence of
the grapes in the background, to which he has added a decorative leaf
pattern.

PIAZZETTA, GIOVANNI BATTISTA
1683–1754, Italian. *The Drummer*
Black and white chalk on gray paper, 20½ × 15⅜ in.
Museo Correr, Venice, Toso photo

Here is one of Piazzetta's heads for which he was justly famous. These
drawings were finished art works and not studies for paintings.
Piazzetta was a leading Venetian painter during his time and the first
director of the Venice Academy at its beginning in 1750. This young
boy must have been a favorite of the artist, for he used him as a model
in many of his works.

RUBENS, PETER PAUL
1577–1640, Flemish
Seated Nude Youth
C. 1614
Black and white chalk drawing
19⅞ × 11¹³⁄₁₆ in.
The Pierpont Morgan Library
New York

This powerful study for Rubens'
painting *Daniel in the Lions' Den*
is packed with energy and vigor.
The artist had already roughed
out the painting in oil, and here is
concentrating in a drawing on
developing the figure of Daniel.
The massiveness of the youth's
shoulders and the large hands all
the more accentuate his pious and
imploring facial expression.

RUBENS. *Youthful Self-Portrait.* Oil
John G. Johnson Collection, Philadelphia

Dutch painters were exceedingly fond of self-portraits. This one of
Rubens was done very early in his career and illustrates just how young
talent could express itself.

TERBRUGGHEN, HENDRICK, 1588–1629, Dutch. *Flute Player*, 1621
Oil on canvas, 27½ × 21⅝ in. *Kunstsammlungen, Kassel, Germany*

Terbrugghen was in Rome while Caravaggio was still there. His
favorite subjects were Caravaggiesque young boys in musical poses:
playing the flute or stringed instruments, and singing.

TERBRUGGHEN. *Boy Singing*, 162?. Canvas, 33½ × 28¼ in.
Museum of Fine Arts, Boston

Intent and earnest, this youthful singer is shown with his right hand
raised beating the rhythm, while his left holds the songbook. This was
the conventional singing pose of the day.

REMBRANDT HARMENSZ. VAN RIJN, 1606–1669
Dutch. *Self-Portrait as a Youth,* 1629
Panel, 14¾ × 11½ in. *Mauritshuis Museum, The Hague*

Rembrandt painted himself so many times and at all stages of his life
(more than one hundred times) that these portraits form a pictorial
biography of this greatest of all Dutch painters. Painted when he was
only twenty-three, this portrait reveals a youthful self-confidence and
assurity in contrast with his middle-age portraits, which register
disillusionment and weariness with the troubles and sufferings he
experienced in his personal life.

112

VERMEER, JOHANNES REYNIERSZ, 1632–1675
Dutch. *Portrait of a Young Boy.* Oil on canvas, 23¼ × 19¾ in.
The Metropolitan Museum of Art, New York
The Jules S. Bache Collection, 1949

Many, but not all, critics attribute this painting to Vermeer. It shows
the head of an attractive boy with full lips and a fairly large nose.
Across his shoulders is thrown a loosely blown mantle. The left eye
seems to be looking directly at the viewer, but the right eye is glancing
sideways, thus achieving a rather startling effect.

VELDE, ADRIAEN VAN DE, 1636–1672, Dutch
Studies of a Shepherd Boy. Chalk drawing. *Stedelijk Museum, Amsterdam*

One of the most noted landscape artists in Dutch painting, Van de Velde often filled his pastoral landscapes with young shepherds and herdsmen. Here are two very likable poses of a young shepherd, one looking off into space, the other glancing down at his leg and lost in contemplation.

opposite:
CUIJP (CUYP), AELBERT, 1620–1691. Dutch. *Boy with Falcon* Oil, 29¾ × 25 in. *The Metropolitan Museum of Art, New York George T. Delacorte, Jr., Fund, 1957*

Cuijp was mainly a landscape painter. In 1651, when he was thirty-one, he painted a remarkable work called *Poultry*, but this type of painting was rare for him. He also did a few portraits, of which this has been identified as one. Even here he can't resist introducing a bird along with his proud and dressed-to-the-hilt young man.

114

115

RIBERA, JUSEPE DE, 1591–1652, Spanish. *St. Sebastian,* 1636
Philadelphia Museum of Art, Philadelphia, Wilstach Collection

Using the style of Caravaggio and his chiaroscuro technique, Ribera
has painted this central figure romantically, more in a classical tradition
than as a suffering Christian martyr. While one arrow had penetrated
the body, there are none protruding from it now, thus giving the
muscular body an ethereal quality.

opposite:
VELÁZQUEZ, DIEGO RODRIGUEZ DE SILVA Y, 1599–1660, Spanish
Prince Baltasar Carlos on Horseback, 1634
Canvas, 82¼ × 68 in. *Prado Museum, Madrid*

Spain's first great painter, Velázquez, was court painter to Philip IV
of Spain. One of the court children he worshiped was this young prince,
whom he painted in full ceremonial clothes astride a galloping steed.
This is no stiff portrait, but one of staggering freedom, and perhaps the
first portrait of a child on horseback done in the grand manner.

116

ZURBARÁN, FRANCISCO DE
1598–1664, Spanish
The Christ Child, late 1630s
Oil on wood, 16½ × 18½ in.
Pushkin Museum of Fine Arts, Moscow

This Baroque painter was known for his
religious subjects and for his interest in
painting children. He has pictured a
young Christ child as a realistic
youngster who might just as well have
been any other innocent child on the
streets of Seville, Spain. It was painted
as part of an altarpiece of the Trinitarian
Church in Seville.

MURILLO, BARTOLOMÉ ESTEBAN
1617–1682, Spanish
St. Thomas of Villa Nueva Dividing
His Clothes Among the Beggar Boys
Cincinnati Art Museum
Cincinnati, Ohio
Gift of Mrs. Mary E. Emery

This anecdotal subject was dear to the
hearts of Murillo's countrymen. The
young saint seems to be enjoying the
fruits of giving, while the beggar boys
have expressions of amazed delight,
gratitude, and openly smiling joy at their
unexpected windfall.

MURILLO
The Beggar Boy
C. 1646
Louvre Museum, Paris

This type of portrait of a ragamuffin
brought Murillo overnight fame and
popularity. The Spanish people
immediately took to his tender, touching,
somewhat effeminate young boys.

EL S DᴺMANVEL OSORÍO MANRRIQVE D ZVÑIGA S¹ᴵᴺ GINES NACIO EN Nᵗ A¹¹ E¹¹ 1784

GOYA. *Boys Inflating a Bladder.* Canvas, $45^5/8 \times 48^7/8$ in. *Prado Museum, Madrid*

opposite:
GOYA Y LUCIENTES, FRANCISCO JOSÉ, 1746–1828, Spanish
Don Manuel Osorio de Zuñiga, 1784. Oil on canvas, 59 × 40 in.
The Metropolitan Museum of Art, New York
Jules S. Bache Collection, 1949

Goya was designated the official painter of the Spanish king in
July, 1786. It was natural, then, that he did many portraits of royal
personages, including youngsters, although he is far better known today
for his political and military works.

Martin Freminet de paris

FRÉMINET, MARTIN
1564–1619, French
Young Man Wearing Cap with Feather
Pen and red chalk drawing
Albertina Museum, Vienna

This artist was both a painter to Henry IV
and drawing teacher to Louis XIII. Only
a few of his paintings survive, the most
famous being the ceiling of the Chapel
of the Trinity at Fontainebleau. The
draftsman was obviously in the same
frivolous mood as his subject matter, for
he has the cat, who is crouched under
the pert young man's right leg, playing
a violin. The rakish hat on the youth's
head with its elongated feather adds to
the mood of sophisticated merriment.

WATTEAU, JEAN-ANTOINE
1684–1721, French
*Three Studies of the Head
of a Young Negro*, c. 1715
Black and red chalk drawing
with whitewash, 9½ × 10⅝ in.
*Louvre Museum, Paris
Cabinet des Dessins*

Watteau was seriously attracted to racial
and exotic types. He used this particular
young Negro boy as his model many
times and did several versions of this
drawing. These three heads are considered
to be one of his most brilliant
achievements; certainly they are among
the most enjoyed and most popular in
the history of art.

CHARDIN, JEAN-BAPTISTE-SIMÉON
1699–1779, French. *Child with Top*
Canvas, 22⅞ × 29⅞ in. *Louvre Museum, Paris*

This perfectionist worked long and hard to achieve the rigid esthetic standards in which he believed. In this portrait, considered one of his masterpieces, Chardin endows this boy with a beautiful face expressive both of adolescent wisdom and understanding. It was exhibited at the Salon in 1738, where its viewers were immediately impressed with the fastidious yet simple dress of the boy and his boyish interest in the spinning top.

PERRONEAU, JEAN-BAPTISTE, 1715–1783, French. *Boy with Book*
Oil, 28¾ × 24⅜ in. *Hermitage Museum, Leningrad*

One of this pastelist's finest oil portraits, this work was exhibited at the
Paris Salon in 1746. It is of a young schoolboy whom the painter
apparently knew well and enjoyed painting. The boy's fleeting expression
is subtly drawn, and his instant reaction, almost one of surprise at being
discovered reading a book, is charming. This artist was among those
known as itinerant painters. They would go from country to country,
town to town, announcing their prices and that they were there for
assignments, and paint whoever wanted their portraits done.

GREUZE, JEAN-BAPTISTE
1725–1805, French
Child with an Apple
National Gallery, London

Greuze was both a painter of genre and
portraits, the latter especially in the
children's field, where he concentrated
on expressing purity and innocence. As
in this appealing portrait, he uses delicate
flesh tones to achieve a particularly
intriguing sensuousness, even in one so
young.

GREUZE
*Portrait of a Young Man
in a Three-Cornered Hat*
Oil, 24 × 19¹¹/₁₆ in.
Hermitage Museum, Leningrad

Because he was held in high esteem by
Catherine the Great and Czar Paul I,
many of Greuze's portraits found their
way to Russia. The artist, preferring the
Dutch and Flemish style to that of his
own country, rendered this young man
with a similarity to Rembrandt in the
lighting and in the chiaroscuro treatment.

125

CLODION (CLAUDE MICHEL)
1738–1814, French
Bacchant. Marble, 67 × 22 × 26⅛ in.
National Gallery of Art, Washington, D.C.
Samuel H. Kress Collection

Clodion's decorative Rococo style was
at its peak of popularity in the 1780s, a
few years prior to the French Revolution.
It was an age of frivolous decadence and
artificial gaiety when art was an adjunct
of the boudoir and the salon. No wonder
the aristocracy loves this sculptor's erotic
statuettes of nymphs, fauns, and
bacchantes. These he carved as if the
marble was as soft as flesh itself and the
bodies as lush as the luxuriant living of
the ill-fated times.

126

CHAUDET, ANTOINE DENIS, 1763–1810, French
L'Amour. Louvre Museum, Paris

Chaudet studied in Rome and was greatly influenced by Canova, but
he added an excessive amount of sentimentality and sweetness to his
figures, as in the dainty manner in which this winged boy holds the bee
and the rose, while on the base little cherubs shoot arrows into the
beehive.

127

COPLEY, JOHN SINGLETON, 1738–1815, American
Midshipman Augustus Brine, 1782. Oil on canvas, 50 × 40 in.
The Metropolitan Museum of Art, New York
Richard De Wolfe Brixey Bequest, 1943

Although American, Copley settled in England in 1775 and gave his full time to portraits and historical canvases. He had already achieved fame for his colonial American portraiture.

HOPPNER, JOHN
C. 1758–1810, English
Richard Humphreys, the Boxer
Oil on canvas, 55¾ × 44¼ in.
The Metropolitan Museum of Art
New York
Alfred N. Punnett Fund, 1953

One of England's better-known portrait painters has captured a typical boxing stance of "The Gentleman Boxer who was never conquered." He is here pictured full-length, somewhat less than life-size, stripped to the waist. When he fought the "Bath Butcher" at Newmarket on May 3, 1786, the match was attended by the Prince of Wales and the Dukes of York and Orléans.

PEAKE, ROBERT, THE ELDER
C. 1576–1616. English
Henry Frederick, Prince of Wales,
and Sir John Harrington, 1603
Oil on canvas, 79½ × 58 in.
The Metropolitan Museum of Art,
New York
Joseph Pulitzer Bequest

As the title of this painting indicates, Peake was a famous portraitist of royal personages. Among his better-known works was a portrait of Prince Charles prior to his becoming Charles I of England. In his later years he enjoyed a large share of the patronage of the younger nobility and of the young members of the court. The landscaped background against which these two youths are set is remarkably detailed, as is the horse with all his vestments.

129

BLAKE, WILLIAM, 1757–1827, English. *Angel Binds the Dragon*
Engraving, 14¼ × 12¹³/₁₆ in.
Fogg Art Museum, Harvard University, Cambridge, Massachusetts
Gift of W. A. White

Here is an example of Blake's imaginative use of the young male nude
inspired by a revival of interest in England at that time in the works
of Michelangelo. His well-known utterance, "all forms are perfected in
the poet's mind," is well illustrated by this heroic male's powerful
body, his fiercely intent expression in the eyes, and his poetically
sensuous mouth.

130

BLAKE. *Glad Day*, 1780. Colored print. 10 × 7¹⁄₂ in.
British Museum, London

Going back directly to the Vitruvian-man concept of figure drawing,
Blake added the beauty and vitality of the Hellenistic Apollos to this
spiritually radiant figure of Albion descending from the heavens and
landing lightly on his left foot on the earth. An illustration for one of
Blake's verses, it invites the viewer to accept the poet's optimism and
sincere belief in life's values.

131

FLANDRIN, HIPPOLYTE, 1809–1864, French
Study of a Male Nude, 1885. 38½ × 48¾ in. *Louvre Museum, Paris*

A student and follower of Ingres, Flandrin was never known for any particular style of his own, but he did leave for posterity's acclaim this one painting of a totally sensuous young male nude that understandably has been one of the most popular attractions at the Louvre.

PART IV

In the Nineteenth Century

Jacques-Louis David was not only the painter of the French Revolution and the dictator of art in France, he was also the painter of the Napoleonic era. Louis XIV had been replaced by a Republic, whose armies were led by Napoleon Bonaparte, who soon in turn elevated his power to that of Emperor. But by 1814 the combined forces of England, Germany, and Russia had soundly defeated him and caused him to be sent into exile.

How did these political and military events affect the trends in art at the beginning of the nineteenth century? The French Revolution had abruptly put an end to the Baroque and Rococo eras in art, to be replaced by a Neoclassicism, of which David was the chief proponent. Napoleon furthered this course by considering himself as a modern ancient Roman Emperor. Since David had become an ardent supporter of the Emperor, it was logical that all art was dominated by this Neoclassic style. In particular, while David himself did not paint the many male nudes of this period, his emphasis on classical themes paved the way for them. It was for his pupil and follower, Jean-Auguste-Dominique Ingres, to become the supreme master of the academic classic nude figure. His study for *The Golden Age* was just one of four hundred and fifty this classic perfectionist did in preparation for his famous work. The nudes of Ingres were not of a sensuous nature, but they were severely disciplined drawings, for Ingres believed that if a work were well drawn, it could then be well painted.

Neoclassicism was enhanced by the archaeological findings of this period in history. Excavations which were carried out at Pompeii and Herculaneum during the latter part of the eighteenth century had revealed the incredible beauty of Greco-Roman art. Politically the French Republic was likened to the Republican sentiment of the Greek and Roman societies. The situation was thus somewhat similar to the Renaissance. In Italy Antonio Canova was considered the world's leading sculptor and his *Perseus* pure Neoclassic. This statue was commissioned by the Vatican to replace the *Apollo Belvedere*, which had been stolen by Napoleon. Far to the north in Copenhagen, Albert Bertel Thorwaldsen was also re-creating Hellenistic sculptures. In England painter William Etty joined the Royal Academy School in 1807 and thereafter devoted his life to the portrayal of the nude in the nonsensuous, classical manner, thereby shocking the English public into at last joining the mainstream of world art.

Returning once again to France, now the world's cultural center, not all the art of the Napoleonic era was Neoclassic. In direct contrast, and inspired to some extent by the exploits of Napoleon on the battlefields, a new school of painting developed known as Romanticism. Influenced by the study of Leonardo in Italy, Prud'hon, a pupil of David, turned to the Romantic. Théodore Géricault in 1812 painted a dashing, swashbuckling portrait of a typical Napoleonic soldier, packed with violent excitement, and with these brushstrokes established at the age of twenty-one a freedom-of-form art movement completely at variance with that of David and Ingres. These Romanticists painted emotion for emotion's sake, rejecting all the standard formulas of the Academy, especially the dogmatic rigidity of drawing. Instead they substituted whatever individual painting techniques the artist cared to use to produce violently romantic and emotionally heightened canvases. The Romanticists not only shocked the members of the staid Academy, but the public itself. Géricault's *Raft of Medusa*, 1819, portrayed a disgraceful shipwreck episode that the French government was trying desperately to keep from public attention, and became a politically controversial painting in addition to being artistically so. The subject of the painting attacked the standing of the military, who should never have let the unseaworthy ship sail, and the portrayal of the gory agony of the dying men on the raft offended the French public's sense of human dignity. Yet, the Napoleonic Wars having left the people discouraged and disillusioned, the public did welcome the painters of the Romantic movement as a much-needed outlet for the expression of their emotional hangups.

By its very nonintellectual approach Romanticism could not last long, and by the middle of the nineteenth century a reaction set in with the flourishing of a Realist school of painters. Economically the world had entered the machine age with the development of steam. Inventions and scientific advances came tumbling one over another, changing the whole complexion of both the economic and art world. Cheap goods flooded the markets of the world due to mass-production processes. Cities and towns grew increasingly larger, and along with their growth came slums. Less emphasis was placed on the creative arts and the artists, as material matters loomed larger on the new industrial class's horizons. Patrons of artists were becoming fewer, and what art the new wealthy industrialists bought was purchased on the basis of the recommendations of a conservative Academy. The new and experimenting artists were pushed aside into a world of their own, virtually disowned by a materialistic society and, unless independently wealthy, forced into a life of poverty in a garret. At first, the Realists painted scenes of the sordid life of the slums they saw all around them and of the frantic efforts of the masses of people to overcome their poverty and achieve some of the benefits which the machine age was dangling before their eyes. Honoré Daumier was in his paintings and caricatures the little peoples' most eloquent spokesman. However grotesque his figures, his human beings were full of warmth and appeal.

The late sixties of the nineteenth century were now ripe for a whole new school of Realist painting and a complete innovation in the techniques and approaches to painting. The artist who founded this new style and thereby started the modern movement in art was Édouard Manet. He believed with the Realist school that an artist should paint what he actually saw, but he went further by stressing the importance of color and light. The chemical industry was beginning to make available startling bright new pigments which Manet and his contemporaries splashed vividly with bold strokes on their canvases. With another bold stroke these artists turned their attention to light, maintaining that the dullest subject could be made beautiful by the proper use of light. By proper use, they meant another new approach, one where the subject matter of the painting was caught at a single instant when light hit it. The complete work thus became an impression rather than a detailed painting, and thus the name Impressionism was given to this brilliant new style.

Naturally the Academy was horrified. Again the traditional rules of a well-drawn academic figure were being ignored and a blatant permissiveness in painting substituted. Still sticking to their interest in Neoclassicism, the public as well as the Academy were shocked. In place of empty and dull nudes, Manet was painting everyday living figures. Two of his paintings, *Olympia* and *The Picnic on the Grass,* with a totally nude woman seated next to two fully clothed and disinterested young men, incurred the wrath of Napoleon III and was deemed to insult public morals. Émile Zola, however, came to their defense and became a vociferous champion of their cause. But Paris and the world was not yet ready for these questionable situations of sexual irregularities and many of Manet's works were destroyed by his infuriated enemies.

Another famous Impressionist and close friend of Manet was Edgar Degas. Chiefly known for his scenes of show business and ballet dancers (all painted indoors), the example shown in this book is on a somewhat different subject, being based on a classic theme which he also often used, the detail from *Young Spartan Girls Challenging Spartan Boys.* Degas came from a wealthy family and therefore had the advantage of being able to paint exactly what and how he wanted. He was immediately attracted to the greater naturalism and the unusual uses of color, tones, and plays of light of the Impressionists. But he combined these with an adherence to the draftmanship of Ingres. In fact, it was just such looseness of drawing and liberty in applying paints with short brushstrokes and quick dabs that brought on a reaction against the methods of the Impressionists, if not their results. A Neo-Impressionism resulted, best shown in the works of Georges Seurat.

Having an extremely mathematical mind and feeling that more permanence was needed in painting than the Impressionists deemed necessary, Seurat developed a method called Pointillism. Very meticulously he arranged hundreds of colored dots according to a strict geometrical pattern; an outstanding example of this technique is his *Bathers,* 1886. Another, for a time, Neo-Impressionist painter was Paul Gauguin, who during his sojourns in Polynesia turned for his inspiration to primitive cultures and exploitation of the mysteries of exoticism.

In the early 1870s another Impressionist painter appeared on the scene, who, as no other artist, was to influence the entire trend of modern art, Paul Cézanne. During this decade he painted brilliantly lit outdoor scenes, as had Manet. But he soon became dissatisfied with the limitations of Impressionism, and in 1880 became the first post-Impressionist. To the instantaneous paintings of the Impressionists he brought the solid qualities of such masters of the Italian Renaissance as Masaccio and Michelangelo. He simplified nature in the shape of his objects and deliberately drew proportions which were unreal to nature. Yet the results always looked just right. That, he insisted, was because a painting had laws of its own that were unlike the laws of nature, but as he used them they were exactly right for his wanted effect. Cézanne, too, distorted his subject matter, even more so than his contemporaries.

It is difficult to use the end of one century and the beginning of another as a sharp dividing line between schools of painting or the works of artists themselves. So many of the giants of the end of the nineteenth century were also giants of the early years of the twentieth century. Among the many other accepted painters in this group could be listed Henri de Toulouse-Lautrec, Henri Rousseau, and James Ensor. All of these artists created many important works featuring the young male in art.

While painting dominated the cultural scene of the nineteenth century, the seeds of modern sculpture were being sown in Germany by Adolf Hildebrand and in France by Auguste Rodin, two realists whose works and plastic principles were to profoundly shape the sculptures to come in the twentieth century. From Belgium came an early modern sculptor, Georges Minne, who added a delicate feminine sensitiveness to his carvings of young males.

NINETEENTH–CENTURY PAINTING IN AMERICA

Unlike Europe the young American nation possessed no cultural heritage. The first settlers on these shores and for generations later had all they could do to establish themselves on a new continent. True, they came from Europe, but they brought with them cows and chickens rather than works of art. Craftsmen in utilitarian trades came over on the first boats, but their energies were devoted to furniture and cabinetmaking, not to emulating the paintings and sculptures of a land from which they had just emigrated. There were, of course, in colonial days some few itinerant portrait painters, but, until after the American Revolution, the colonists were more deeply concerned with the establishment of a political and economic stability than with the building up of a cultural heritage. Of the colonial painters the greatest was John Singleton Copley of Boston, whose portraits, as might be expected, were done after the English portrait school of that time.

From the Revolution to about 1820 this period in American history was known as the Federal era and was dominated by the members of the Federalist party, who ruled American politics. It logically followed that the egos of these leaders would cause them to want their portraits painted for posterity, especially the Presidents of the United States. Most of the American portrait painters of this Federalist period had studied in Europe and then returned to the United States, bringing with them the formal Neoclassicism then in vogue abroad. One famous American portraitist of this time was Rembrandt Peale, whose works showed a close affinity to those of David.

In addition to formal portrait painting three other trends in art activities were being followed in the first half of the nineteenth century in the United States. One was folk art, a primitive form of craftsmanship practiced mostly by itinerant portrait painters, whose most famous exponent was Ammi Phillips. But with the coming of industrialization and the growth of more academic forms of painting, folk art soon began to vanish, eased out by the introduction of the daguerreotype. The second trend was a result of the spread of Europe's Romantic movement to America in the form of landscape painting, begun by Thomas Cole and carried on by the Hudson River school of painting. The third form of painting expression of this period was the patriotic historical works, especially prevalent from the Federal era to the mid-century.

Important changes developed in America by mid-century as a growing middle class and the Democratic Party superseded the Federalists with their portraiture and historical paintings. Anecdotal painting was born. Now what became popular were landscape scenes peopled with recognizable homey and casual figures from around the countryside. In William Sidney Mount those who bought and enjoyed such paintings found their champion. To wonderfully detailed country backgrounds he added recognizable people, especially young farm boys. His works formed a poetry of rural America expressed on canvas.

As the Civil War radically changed the economic composition of the nation, so it did the progress of the arts. Victory for the North meant a triumph for industrialization. Big corporations and financial manipulations were the order of the day. The growth of urban centers with their attendant slums changed America from a pastoral and agricultural nation to a smoke-filled industrial one. Again in America, as abroad, interest in artists and their works was pushed into the background as visions of material wealth and its attainment became full-time occupations for urban industrialists, as well as for prospectors, frontiersmen, and cattle ranchers. Artists by mid-century had become reporters. With the introduction of new printing methods, they found they could earn far more money by painting originals that would then be transferred into an engraving for use in a magazine or book than by painting a single work for an individual patron. The leading such painter, and perhaps the most popular American painter ever born, was Winslow Homer. He was an absolute realist, a storyteller painter, who faithfully reported what he saw in nature and the events of daily life. Reproductions of his works appeared often in *Ballou's Pictorial* and *Harper's Weekly,* for whom he was their Civil War art reporter. Later in the century, after study trips to Paris and London, he retired to Prout's Neck in Maine where he painted so many of his Yankee sea scenes and local people.

Eventually most American painters found their way to various parts of Europe and were influenced accordingly. One, John Singer Sargent, was born abroad and never saw the shores of the United States until his twenties. Another was Thomas Eakins, possibly the second, after Homer, most renowned American painter of his time. During his sojourn in Europe from 1866 to 1869 he learned painting in the best of the European traditions and, thus fortified, returned to America to paint realistically the local Philadelphia people and the scenes he knew so well, be it a prizefighter, wrestler, a boat race on the river, or portraits of his friends. Whereas Homer painted nature and people as he saw them, Eakins went much further by industriously studying anatomy in order to render his figures with absolute and intellectual fidelity to body structure. For this reason, his male nudes constitute the finest ever painted; for not only was he faithful to the actual physical formations of the body, but he endowed them with a passionate emotionalism that was seething within himself and bursting for release. A follower of the Eakins and Homer styles was Robert Henri, who favored, however, a more abstract style.

Three European art centers seemed to attract American artists the most: Paris, of course, then Munich and Düsseldorf. Many were caught up in the French Impressionist furor, among them William Morris Hunt, John La Farge, George Inness, Eastman Johnson, and Alexander Harrison. Others came into contact with the Munich school which followed the styles of Courbet, Manet, and the seventeenth-century Dutch painters. These included Frank Duveneck, who had his own school in Munich, William Merritt Chase, and J. Frank Currier.

For all this activity, however, the lot of the artist in America at the end of the nineteenth century was hardly a lucrative one.

DAVID, JACQUES-LOUIS
1748–1825, French
Portrait of an Unknown Young Man
C. 1800. Oil on canvas, 21¼ × 18½ in.
Pushkin Museum of Fine Arts, Moscow

During the eighteenth century in French
art a certain pictorial freedom was
in vogue in portraiture as opposed to a
hitherto more rigid formality of
presentation. David makes use of this
freer style in this portrait of a shaggy-
haired young man with an alert and
glowing expression, all the more
sensualized by the covetous contours of
his mouth.

opposite:
DAVID. *Colosse de Monte Cavallo.* Drawing. *Louvre Museum, Paris*

After the French Revolution, David returned French art to the classicism
of the Greeks. For this drawing he went to the statuary of the Colossi
of Monte Cavallo in Athens. Especially characteristic of this Phidias
period of Greek sculpture were the massive chests and bulging
abdominal muscles of the monumental human figures, which David has
captured in this towering, almost overpowering nude form.

139

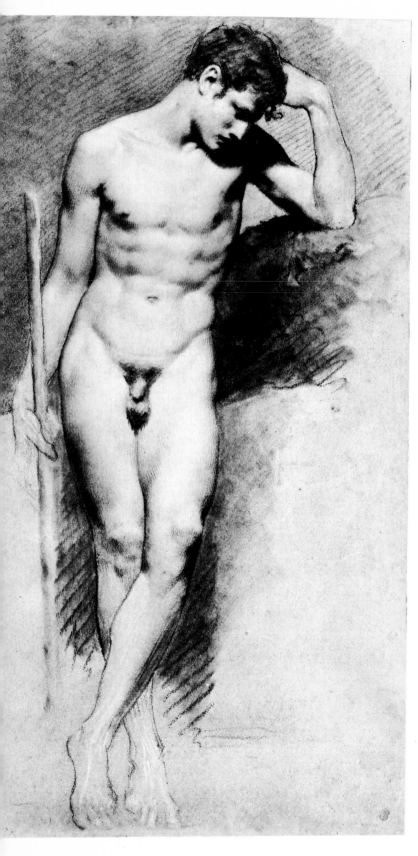

PRUD'HON, PIERRE-PAUL
1758–1823, French
Study of a Nude Male Figure
Black and white chalk on gray paper
17½ × 9⅞ in.
Musée des Arts Decoratifs, Paris

A close friend of Canova, Prud'hon
avidly studied his works and those of
antique sculpture. His Neoclassical style,
however, is much warmer and human
than that of David, and his nude figure,
as shown here, are much more human;
thus he is closer to the Romantic style to
come than the contemporary
Neoclassicism. He was a master of
drawing the nude figure, both male
and female.

opposite:
INGRES, JEAN-AUGUSTE-DOMINIQUE
1780–1867, French
Two Nudes
a study for "The Golden Age"
Pencil on white paper faded to ivory
Outlined with a stylus
15⅜ × 11 in.
*Fogg Art Museum, Harvard University
Cambridge, Massachusetts
Grenville L. Winthrop Bequest*

While Ingres was a pupil of David, he
more closely emulated the romantic
Classicism of Raphael, and in his pencil
drawings he was very much the realist,
as in this study. This drawing is a study
for two large allegorical panels the artist
was commissioned to do for the Château
de Dampierre of the Duc de Luynes.
The male nude was never used, but it
shows the flowing smoothness of Ingres's
style.

140

GÉRICAULT
Nude Warrior with a Spear
Canvas, 36⅞ × 29¾ in.
National Gallery of Art
Washington, D.C.
Chester Dale Collection

Géricault painted many military and war scenes, none more striking than this powerfully muscular nude.

142

opposite:
GÉRICAULT, THÉODORE
1791–1824, French
The Raft of the "Medusa"
1819. Canvas, 193 × 282 in.
Louvre Museum, Paris

One of only three works shown by Géricault during his lifetime, this painting at first shocked the critics of his day because of its "repulsive realism," then became his most popular work. Géricault was one of the finest of Romantic painters, but he insisted on absolute realism of detail. In preparation for this painting he visited hospitals and morgues to study dying patients and dead bodies. The scene is that of the survivors of the shipwrecked *Medusa*, struggling to be seen and rescued by a passing ship. The stark, naked details, the intense emotions of the dying men, their physical and psychological turmoil make a shocking impact on the viewer.

GÉRICAULT
Portrait of a Young Man
Canvas, 23¼ × 18¾ in.
Fogg Art Museum, Harvard University
Cambridge, Massachusetts
Grenville L. Winthrop Bequest

GÉRICAULT
Alfred Dedreux as a Child
Oil on canvas, 18 × 15 in.
The Metropolitan Museum of Art
New York,
Alfred N. Punnett Fund, 1941

143

BOILLY, LOUIS-LEOPOLD
1761–1845, French
Portrait of a Young Man
John G. Johnson Collection
Philadelphia

This French master specialized in portraits and in genre painting. He did over 5,000 small portraits, mostly in miniature, of which this is one.

MANET, ÉDOUARD
1832–1883, French
Boy with a Sword, c. 1860
Oil on canvas, $51^{5}/_{8} \times 36^{3}/_{4}$ in.
The Metropolitan Museum of Art
New York, gift of Erwin Davis, 1889

This is the type of painting that Émile Zola considered Manet should have stuck to if he had wanted success and acceptance in his time. Ironically, this was one of two of Manet's paintings used by his detractors as brickbats to destroy other works of his. A surprised young man is holding in his two small hands an enormous sword as if wondering what in the world he should do with it. Manet admitted to an affinity with the Spanish masters, such as Velázquez, Murillo, and Goya, and here used to best advantage their precise modeling and restraint.

COROT, JEAN-BAPTISTE-CAMILLE
1796–1875, French. *Italian Peasant Boy*
Canvas, 10 × 12⅞ in.
National Gallery of Art, Washington, D.C.
Chester Dale Collection

Although Corot is mainly famous for
his exquisite landscapes, he painted many
individual figures, especially children.
His style was marked by simplicity and
with great care as to details. His
backgrounds are almost bare and never
used for decorative effect.

DEGAS, HILAIRE GERMAIN EDGAR
1834–1917, French
Achille de Gras in the Uniform of a Cadet
Canvas, 25½ × 20½ in.
National Gallery of Art, Washington, D.C.
Chester Dale Collection

Degas's first paintings were mostly
portraits of his friends. Like most of
them, this one possesses a rigid
formality that recalls Bronzino's *Ludovico
Capponi.*

SEURAT, GEORGES, 1859–1891, French. *The Bathers*, 1884
Canvas, 79 × 118½ in. *National Gallery, London*

One of the leaders of the Impressionist school, Seurat developed an
individual style of painting with tiny dots of pure color (Pointillism).
However, this painting was done before his full reliance on this
technique. It is a quiet, serene scene of youths bathing in the Seine.
They appear very subdued and quite unlike the American boys of
George Bellows swimming in the river around New York. The heat
haze that has enveloped Paris creates a remarkably blurred effect that
causes the boys' figures to stand out in clear definition.

opposite:
CÉZANNE, PAUL, 1839–1906, French. *The Bather*, c. 1885
Oil on canvas, 50 × 38⅛ in.
The Museum of Modern Art, New York, Lillie P. Bliss Collection

This modern artist painted many variations of bathers, also the
favorite subject of a number of his contemporaries. It was not unusual
for Cézanne to highlight the nude figure against a landscaped background,
but in an imaginative portrayal rather than a realistic one. Thus his
paintings were impressions of what he saw—not truly delineated lines.

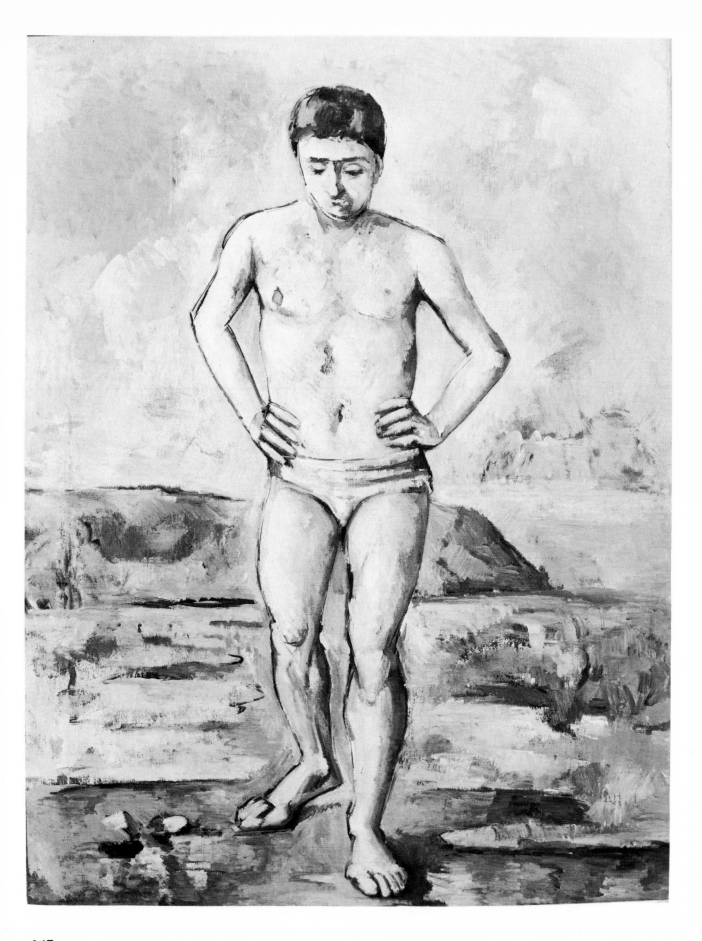

147

ROUSSEAU, HENRI
1844–1910, French
Boy on the Rocks
After 1895
Oil on canvas, 21³/₄ × 18 in.
National Gallery of Art, Washington, D.C.
Chester Dale Collection

Because he had no formal art training,
Rousseau began painting primitive, folk
art scenes, and for these he became
famous. As a musician in the French
Army he traveled to Mexico, where he
was impressed with tropical landscapes
and exotic jungles, which he used
frequently in his paintings. The young
boy illustrates the childlike and geometric
patterns that characterized much of his
work.

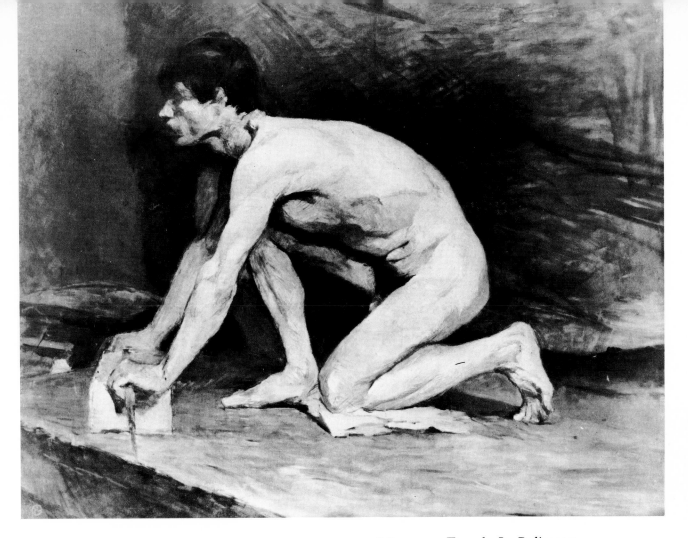

TOULOUSE-LAUTREC, HENRI DE, 1864–1901, French. *Le Polisseur*
C. 1885. Oil on canvas, 25⅝ × 31⅞ in.
Huntington Hartford Collection, New York

Perhaps best-known for his bold and gaudy posters, Toulouse-Lautrec
also painted many athletic scenes, one of which this nude youth might
seem to be part of. From his pose one might expect him to be a sprinter,
but the title of this painting labels him a polisher. He is a shoeshine
boy, grasping in his hand his shoeshine kit.

opposite:
DAUMIER, HONORÉ, 1808–1879, French. *The Young Courier*
Crayon with wash, 6 × 9 in.
National Gallery of Art, Washington, D.C., Rosenwald Collection

While he was most popular for his thousands of cartoons and caricatures,
Daumier was not only an excellent realistic painter, but an accomplished
draftsman, especially of bourgeois subjects. This young boy is running
fast, and is almost out of breath in his feverish haste to accomplish his
mission. His expression is determined and just a bit fearful that he
will be late.

GAUGUIN, PAUL
1848–1903, French
Útěk (detail) Oil on canvas
National Gallery, Prague

During this artist's last years in Tahiti
and the neighboring islands, he painted
many works reminiscent of the fresco
style of painting and that were influenced
by Japanese art, as this one shows. It
illustrates Gauguin's superb talent for
symbolizing exotic and primitive cultures,
but with an added warmth of his own
understanding of these people.

CARPEAUX, JEAN BAPTISTE
1827–1875, French
Neapolitan Fisherboy
Marble, $36\frac{1}{4} \times 16\frac{1}{2} \times 18\frac{3}{8}$ in.
National Gallery of Art, Washington, D.C.
Samuel H. Kress Collection

Having studied with François Rude,
Carpeaux went on to free the sculpture
of his day from its conventional static
state and give it fluidity and lifelikeness.
That he succeeded in putting animation
and vitality in his work can be seen in
this utterly charming nude boy with his
captivating mischievous expression.

opposite:
GAUGUIN
Te Tiare Farani
Oil, $28\frac{3}{4} \times 36\frac{3}{16}$ in.
Pushkin Museum of Fine Arts, Moscow

Gauguin arrived in Tahiti in the middle
of 1891 and was immediately impressed
with this strange land, its people, and
all he saw around him. His exuberance
manifests itself in this contrasting scene
of the lazy, vacuous-looking boy in the
left foreground and the eager, anticipating
expression on the face appearing in the
window.

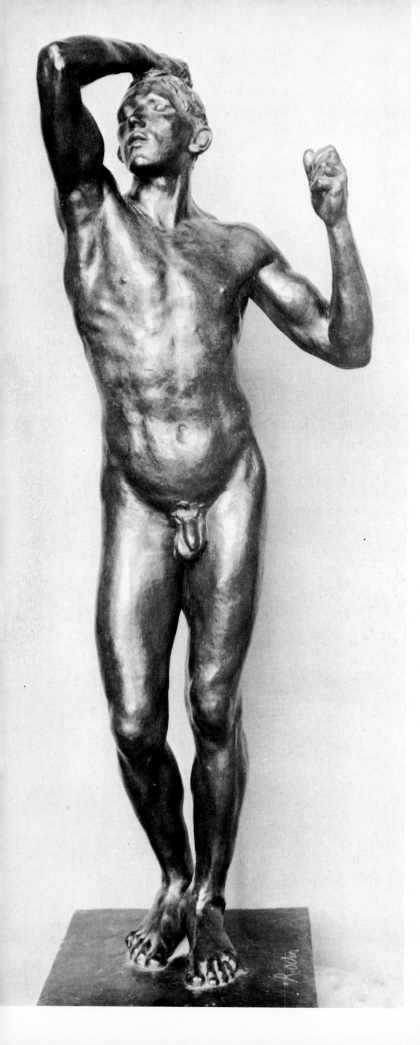

RODIN, AUGUSTE
1840–1917, French
Age of Bronze, 1876. Bronze
Musée Rodin, Paris

Known today as the father of modern
sculpture, Rodin, an unknown in 1875
when he made a trip to Italy, was
greatly influenced by Michelangelo and
his depiction of the young male nude in
sculpture. On his return to France he
picked as a model a handsome young
army man, and in the span of eighteen
months produced this famous *Age of
Bronze.* So lifelike was it, that he was
accused of casting it directly from a
human form. It was not until 1880 that
it was recognized for what it was really
worth and bought by the French
government.

opposite:
RODIN
The Prodigal Son
Before 1889
Bronze, ht. 4 ft., 6¾ in.
Musée Rodin, Paris

The vehemence and dramatic pose of
this sculpture makes it one of Rodin's
most powerful works. Into it he has put
his most expressive sentiments about
humanity and their sufferings.

153

CANOVA, ANTONIO
1757–1822, Italian
The Tarnowska Perseus
Marble, ht. 7 ft., 6 in.
*The Metropolitan Museum of Art
New York, Fletcher Fund, 1967*

Canova, the leading art authority of his
day, was at the height of his fame when
he carved this Perseus. It is a frankly
sensuous rendition, whose body has the
smoothness and fullness of the artist's
Venus Victrix. As a leader in the
Neoclassic movement, he patterned his
subjects and style on the ancient
Greek statues and Greek mythology.

154

OLIVIER, FRIEDRICH, 1791–1859, German. *Young Man Playing
the Flute*, c. 1821
Pencil drawing. *Landeshauptstadt Art Museum, Düsseldorf*

This self-taught artist painted portraits and landscapes while working in
Italy with a group of German writers and artists known as the
Nazarenes, whose object was to revive the religious spirit of the past,
especially as expressed in the works of Dürer. Later he returned to
Munich, where he painted some of the halls in the Munich Castle.

155

BÖCKLIN, ARNOLD, 1827–1901, Swiss. *Shepherd's Lament,* 1866
54¼ × 39¼ in. *Bayernschen Staatsgemäldesammlungen, Munich*

A forerunner of German Expressionism, Böcklin, along with Hans von
Marées, belonged to the school of German Romanticism. Known for
his allegorical compositions, he combined mythical classical scenes with
down-to-earth figures, such as this nude boy. While very successful in
his own day, after his death his works were considered trite and overly
sentimental.

ENSOR, JAMES, 1860–1949, Belgian. *The Lamp Boy*, 1880
Oil on canvas, 59¾ × 35¾ in. *Royal Museum of Fine Arts, Brussels*

An innovator of radical art into Belgium and a forerunner of the German Expressionist movement to come, Ensor's works were enigmatic and somewhat fantastic. He often used local Ostend youngsters as his models, as in this first canvas of his to gain official recognition.

MARÉES, HANS VON
1837–1887, German
Man Leading a Horse with Nymph
and detail, 1881
Kunsthalle, Hamburg

A forerunner of the German Expressionist
school, Marées delighted in mixing the
romantic with the classical. This
mythical, pagan scene sets nude young
men and women in an idyllic background,
with the artist's favorite subject, the horse,
playing an important role. It is at once
natural and idealistic in feeling.

MARÉES. *Standing Male Nude.* Charcoal drawing, heightened with white on gray paper
Staatliche Graphische Sammlung, Munich

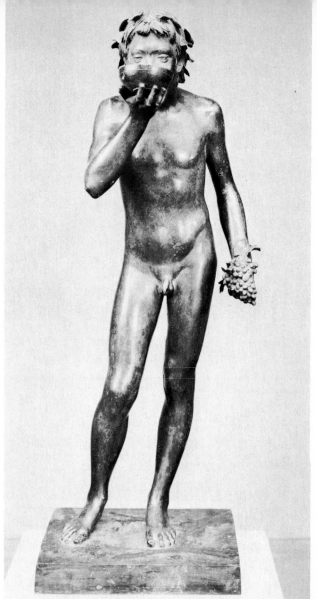

HILDEBRAND, ADOLF E. R. VON
1847–1921, German
The Wine Bearer
1870–1872. Bronze, ht. 33¼ in.
Staatliche Museen, Berlin

Perhaps the father of modern German sculpture, Hildebrand exerted an important influence on the sculptors who followed him. He revived many of the attributes of the sculpture of the Renaissance, especially its harmony, simplicity, and pure form, as personified in this nude youth drinking wine from a bowl while symbolically holding a bunch of ripe grapes in his left hand.

THORWALDSEN, ALBERT BERTEL
1768/70–1844, Danish
Mercury about to Kill Argus
1818. Marble, ht. 67¼ in.
Thorwaldsens Museum, Copenhagen

A contemporary of Canova, Thorwaldsen is best known for the excess romanticism he added to his treatment of Archaic Greek figures. This rendering of the mythical Greek god about to kill the never-sleeping giant Argus is the sculptor's most important work.

BISSEN, HERMANN WILHELM, 1798–1868, Danish. *Akilleus*
Ny Carlsberg Glyptotek, Copenhagen

Bissen was the most faithful of all Thorwaldsen's pupils and assistants, but he outlived his master to create works that showed his own independence. From 1824 to 1834 he was in Rome studying the classic sculptures and working in the style of Thorwaldsen. When the master died, Bissen did three colossal statues from drawings left by Thorwaldsen for the Christiansborg Palace courtyard. *Akilleus* shows how very attuned Bisson was to the classical idiom.

MANCINI, ANTONIO
1852–1930, Italian
*The Standard Bearer
of the Harvest Festival*
Oil on canvas, 65 × 33½ in.
*Isabella Stewart Gardner Museum
Boston*

To achieve just the effect he wanted,
Mancini often mixed grains of glass and
scraps of tin with his paints. This young,
dressed-up standard bearer is one of the
many youths—little acolytes, urchins,
schoolboys, and orphans—that he painted
so well with sentimentality richly
interlaced with realism.

opposite:
ETTY, WILLIAM
1787–1849, English
Male Nude
Royal College of Art, London

Etty was the first English painter to
specialize in the nude figure as his subject
for research and painting. Mostly he
used the female form, but he was equally
at home painting powerful male nudes.
His young men were always virile and
intensely masculine, as can be seen in
this figure study. Prior to the end of the
eighteenth century English artists ignored
the nude. It was left to Etty to bring
beauty, dignity, and strength to this form
of art.

163

BURNE-JONES, SIR EDWARD COLEY
1833–1898, English
The Arming of Perseus
Gouache on canvas, 59½ × 53½ in.
Southampton Art Gallery, Southampton

British art of this period reflected a
bourgeois and Victorian industrialism.
This artist reacted boldly against this by
turning to the recreation of the romantic
figures of the Greek Golden Age and the
Botticelli quest for beauty in the human
form. The two male nudes in this work
are in sharp contrast to the fully clothed
females.

SKOVGAARD, JOAKIM, 1856–1933, Danish
Adam Naming the Beasts
C. 1898. Casein, 40 × 89 in. *Statens Museum for Kunst, Copenhagen*

The French revival of religious painting during this period was reflected
in Denmark in the works of two brothers, Joakim and Niels Skovgaard.
Because of his "Viborg style," a combination of old Italian church
art and modern Danish, Joakim Skovgaard was commissioned to paint
the biblical murals in the Viborg Cathedral. This monumental
undertaking took until 1906 to complete.

MINNE, GEORGES, 1866–1941, Belgian. *Kneeling Youth,* 1898
Plaster, ht. 31⅜ in.
The Museum of Modern Art, New York
Gift of Mr. and Mrs. Samuel Josefowitz

Out of his intense interest in medieval art came many of this artist's
works portraying emaciated and mystical young boys. Concentrating
only on nude figures, mainly of young male adolescents, his most
famous work is the *Fountain with Five Kneeling Boys* for the Folkwang
Museum, Hagen, Germany, in which each of the five naked boys is the
same figure repeated. As seen here, his sculptures are filled with
sentiment and piety, his narrow, shaftlike figures full of sensitivity.

MAENTEL, JACOB
1763–1863, American
Boy with Rooster
C. 1815. Watercolor and ink
Henry Francis du Pont
Winterthur Museum
Winterthur, Delaware

A profile portrait that gains added interest because of the contrast between the boy's hair being combed forward while the rooster's tail is combed backward. This rural Pennsylvanian artist liked to accentuate the colorful costumes of his youngsters.

BREWSTER, JOHN, JR.
1766–184?, American
Boy with Finch
C. 1800. Oil
Abby Aldrich Rockefeller
Folk Art Collection
Williamsburg, Virginia

This favorite Connecticut folk art painter was a deaf-mute who could charmingly convey his message on canvas. This crisp, concise portrait could have been that of his own nephew or possibly the son of a traveling physician whom he knew.

PHILLIPS, AMMI
1787 or 1788–1865, American
Robert Lottridge Dorr
C. 1814. Oil
Abby Aldrich Rockefeller
Folk Art Collection
Williamsburg, Virginia

One of the finest of the New England
folk painters, Phillips did this
surprisingly sophisticated rendering of so
young a lad early in his long career.

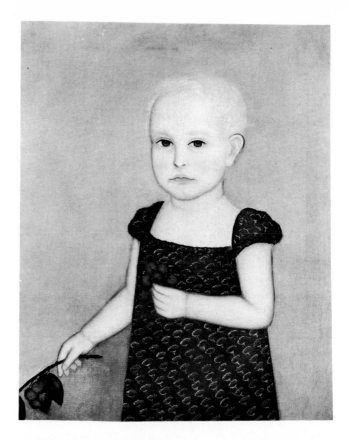

SHEFFIELD, ISAAC
1798–1845, American
Portrait of James Francis Smith
Oil on canvas, 48 × 35½ in.
Lyman Allyn Museum
New London, Connecticut

PEALE, REMBRANDT
1778–1860, American
George Taylor of Philadelphia
The Brooklyn Museum
Brooklyn, New York

One of two painter sons of Charles
Willson Peale, Rembrandt is remembered
in American art history for his many
vigorous portraits of George Washington
and a masterpiece portrait of Thomas
Jefferson. In his detailed style he followed
the school of David. One of his most
charming portraits is this unassuming
youngster holding an arrow in one hand
and a bow in the other.

ALLSTON, WASHINGTON
1779–1843, American
Italian Shepherd Boy, 1819
Oil, 47½ × 34⅛ in.
The Brooklyn Museum
Brooklyn, New York

This artist is considered America's first
romantic painter. During a sojourn in
Italy from 1805 to 1806 he made many
drawings of native figures, one of which
was this young boy. Later he used this
sketch for his painting which he did for
the New England family of William
Gibson Borland. Here he introduces a
dreamlike mood, for the seated boy is
lost in reverie, his partially nude figure
beautifully lighted against the warm but
mystical Faustian background.

SULLY, THOMAS
1783–1872, American
The Torn Hat, 1820
Oil on panel, 19⅛ × 14½ in.
Museum of Fine Arts, Boston

Born in England, Sully on his coming to America studied with Gilbert Stuart in Boston. He painted this red-cheeked boy with exquisitely defined and delicately parted lips. It is one of the artist's best-loved works. The tear in the hat allows the sunshine to come through and brightly reflect on the boy's forehead, while the top part of the face is shaded by the hat itself.

INMAN, HENRY
1801–1846, American
Mumble the Peg, 1842
*The Pennsylvania Academy
of the Fine Arts
Philadelphia*

Inman was a favorite American painter. His portrait of President Martin Van Buren was done for New York's City Hall. His illustrations appeared in leading periodicals of his day: the *Knickerbocker History* and the *Sketch Book.* Among his gracefully composed portrait scenes is this one of two cute youngsters engaged in a very popular game of the nineteenth century, an excellent example of American romantic realism.

169

MOUNT, WILLAM SIDNEY, 1807–1868, American
Boys Caught Napping in a Field, 1848
Oil on canvas, 29 × 36½ in. *The Brooklyn Museum*
Brooklyn, New York

Before America was caught up in the turmoil of the Industrial Revolution,
artists like Mount painted placid country scenes: rural landscapes
peopled with everyday Americans. To such nostalgic scenes he often
added a sense of humor, as with this old man with a cane catching
these youngsters relaxing when they should have been engaged in more
useful pursuits. Mount was deeply concerned with the smallest detail
of background and with achieving just the right expression of mood on
the faces of his homely and rustic characters.

HUNT, WILLIAM MORRIS
1824–1879, American
The Drummer Boy
Museum of Fine Arts, Boston

Hunt was strongly influenced by Millet,
whom he is reputed to have discovered
for America, and by the French Barbizon
school, whose naturalism concerned
itself with the simple and usual aspects
of nature. This subject was a favorite
with Hunt. Here he sets the drummer
boy high above the eye against an
ominous sky and paints him full of
vitality and enthusiasm.

HUNT
The Ball Players
The Detroit Institute of Arts
Detroit, Michigan

With Millet's Impressionism in mind,
Hunt executed this everyday American
scene in a particularly moving
atmospheric background. It fuses his
two painting instincts into one: the
reality of what he saw and the poetic
impressions that he felt.

HOMER, WINSLOW, 1836–1910, American. *Snap the Whip*
1872. Oil, 22 × 36½ in.
The Butler Institute of American Art, Youngstown, Ohio

Homer was a top illustrator for the leading magazines and books of his
times, especially *Harper's Weekly*. However, *Snap the Whip* was an
original oil painting, which he did in two versions. The other version is
now in the Metropolitan Museum of Art, New York. In this romping,
frolicking scene of rustic American schoolboys, Homer painted the
simple joys and innocent natures of typical youngsters of the 1870s.

opposite:
HOMER. *Watermelon Boys*, 1876. Oil, 26 × 39 in.
*Cooper-Hewitt Museum of Decorative Arts and Design
Smithsonian Institution, New York*

Many contemporary critics consider this painting of a black boy and a
white boy eating watermelons together as one of Homer's best. "A
chapter in the life of American boys," wrote art critic George W.
Sheldon.

JOHNSON, JONATHAN EASTMAN, 1824–1906, American
Negro Boy with Flute
National Academy of Design, New York, Brenwasser photo

This American painter's popularity was due to his portraits and genre works, into which he injected a pleasant emotionalism and a poetical lyricism, as with this happily occupied young Negro boy. While visiting Germany in 1849 Johnson was a traveling companion of the painter Leutze, famous for his *Washington Crossing the Delaware.*

BROWN, JOHN GEORGE
1831–1913, American
Allegro and Penseroso. Oil
The Corcoran Gallery of Art
Washington, D.C.

Certain painters become illustrious for a
favorite subject which they paint over
and over again. Just as Murillo liked to
paint street urchins. Brown loved to
depict newsboys and bootblacks.

HENRI, ROBERT
1865–1929, American
Boy with Plaid Scarf
The Detroit Institute of Arts
Detroit, Michigan

Robert Henri followed in the tradition
of Homer and Eakins. While he took an
abstract approach to painting, his results
were purely formal. In this portrait he
was intent on achieving truthfulness as
he saw it. Many of his favorite models
were young Mexican Indians of the
Southwest United States.

DUVENECK, FRANK
1848–1919, American
Whistling Boy
1872. Oil on canvas
Cincinnati Art Museum, Cincinnati, Ohio
Gift of Frank Duveneck

During his stay in Munich, Duveneck carefully studied the styles of Hals, Rembrandt, and Velázquez. There he did this painting of the whistling boy before returning to the United States in 1873. It is characterized by a loose style, in which the boy's face is highlighted and detailed, while the rest of the figure remains sketchy.

CHASE, WILLIAM MERRITT
1849–1916, American
The Whistling Boy
The Detroit Institute of Arts
Detroit, Michigan

In 1872 Chase went to Munich where he spent five years and met and worked with Duveneck. They both painted many figures and portraits in the dark tonality of the Munich school, and both chose the whistling boy as a subject for 175 similar paintings.

HARRISON, THOMAS ALEXANDER, 1853–1930, American
Castles in Spain, 1882. Oil on canvas, 37⅛ × 73⅝ in.
The Metropolitan Museum of Art, New York, 1912

A close friend of Whistler and Sargent, Harrison spent the last fifty years of his life in France, where he died at the age of seventy-seven. He was one of the grand old gentlemen of American painters and dean of American artists in their Montparnasse colony. He painted his first major success in 1881, then in 1882 he did this *Castles in Spain,* which was bought by John G. Johnson of Philadelphia.

opposite:

EAKINS, THOMAS COWPERTHWAITE, 1844–1916, American
Salutat, 1898. Oil, 50 × 40 in.
Addison Gallery of American Art
Phillips Academy, Andover, Massachusetts

Eakins believed, like the Greeks, that the human body was the most beautiful object in the world, especially the nude male. A leader in America's naturalistic movement and once head of the Pennsylvania Academy of the Fine Arts, he was forced to resign this latter position because of his emphasis on drawing nudes from live models. He was particularly partial to painting males in the field of sports. This work is of champion boxer Billy Smith, with several prominent men of the day pictured in the audience.

opposite:

EAKINS. *Wrestlers,* c. 1899. Oil sketch, 40 × 50 in.
Philadelphia Museum of Art, Philadelphia

This oil sketch is a preliminary to Eakins' larger work of the same name, which he originally gave to the National Academy of Design, New York, as his "diploma picture."

176

MACMONNIES, FREDERICK WILLIAM, 1863–1937, American
Boy and Heron, 1892. Bronze
The Corcoran Gallery of Art, Washington, D.C.

This very popular American sculptor originally shocked his Boston
critics with a nude statue of *Bacchante*. While in Paris he produced his
Nathan Hale with the same sensuous softness that he gave to this nude
young boy enveloped in the folds of a huge bird. It is a fanciful
conception, brilliantly done, and erotically exciting.

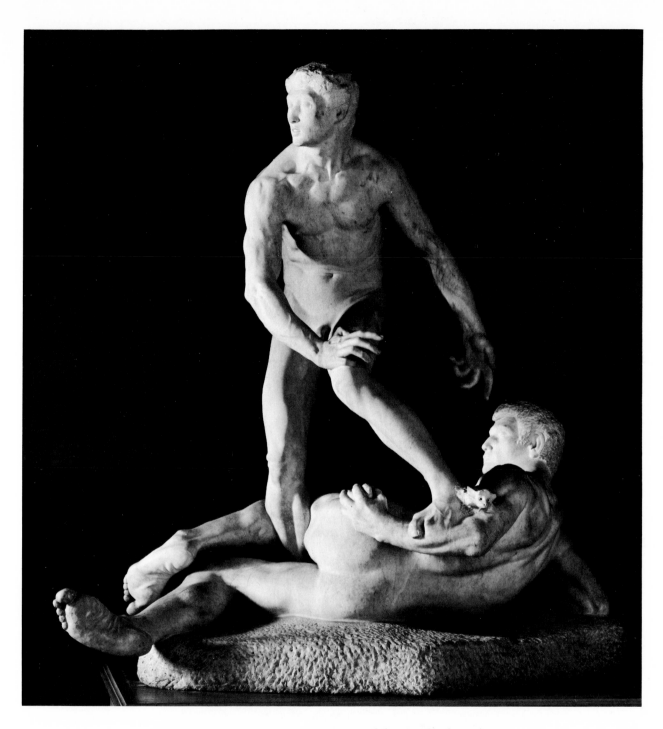

BARNARD, GEORGE GRAY, 1863–1938, American
Struggle of Two Natures in Man, 1894. Marble, ht. 101½ in.
The Metropolitan Museum of Art, gift of Alfred Corning Clark, 1896

A loyal follower of the style of Michelangelo and Rodin, the artist carved this heroic scene directly in stone, after viewing the former's famous slave statues. The figures appear natural but are heightened by the addition of the same idealization of form that Michelangelo used to enhance his works.

INDIAN, C. 1800. *Siva as Mendicant. Museum of Fine Arts, Boston*

PART V

The Exotic Young Male

This section covers the young male in far-off lands and olden times, hence its designation as exotic. Here are gathered together works of art from India, China, Japan, Africa, and pre-Columbian Mexico. They are mainly religious in nature and mostly sculptures, since these cultures represented the young male, if they carved him at all, as statues of religious significance. This was especially true of the Hindu religion in India.

The Hindus of India lived according to a caste system. At the top, and therefore the elite of society, were the priests, followed by warriors, farmers, laborers, and untouchables, in that order. One was born to one of these caste categories and stayed within it all during his life. Thus the priests perpetuated their absolute control over Indian society. The early Hindu religion was known as Brahmanism and stemmed from the recognition of Brahma as the supreme being. He stood for the supreme soul of the universe. But a trinity existed consisting of Brahma and two other dieties: Vishnu, a god linked with the preservation of the world, and Siva, a god of the eternal process of creation and destruction. This triple divinity represented the earthly manifestation of the eternal and infinite soul. In the worship of this concept, final emancipation in afterlife could be gained only upon attaining the perfect knowledge of this divine essence. In representing this religious philosophy in art, at first it was forbidden to use the human form, and symbols were carved in its place. But as the religion became more humane and less mystic, the Brahmans carved in human form the three divinities of the trinity, and many of these statues are in museums all over the world.

Buddhism arose in opposition to the strictness and formality of the Brahman faith. It, too, adhered to the same caste system, with its priests claiming primacy over the rest of the populace. A devout young prince, the Gautama Buddha, left his courtly life and dedicated himself to attaining complete spiritual fulfillment and reaching the goal of attaining perfect divine knowledge. He was supposed to have lived from 563–483 B.C., and after his death cults formed for the purpose of worshiping him as their god and of emulating him in his chosen way of life. However, it was several hundred years later that he was represented in art as a human figure, and then hundreds of statues were carved of Buddha, mostly as impersonal symbols rather than natural human beings.

In the third century B.C. when Indian Emperor Asoka declared Buddhism to be the official religion of the country, Persian sculptors were invited to come to India to practice their art in depicting Buddha. These statues were no longer of the abstract variety, but were youthful Buddha figures in gentle poses full of sensuous rhythm and soft beauty.

Foreign influences on the art of India were few, and even the conquest of northern India by Alexander the Great left little of the Hellenistic culture's impression on the Hindu artists. Thus Indian art developed on its own, and from A.D. 320 to 647 reached its

181

"Golden Age," known as the Gupta period, when the Gupta emperors united all the parts of India which had been under foreign rule, formed a Hindu cultural renaissance, and became great patrons of the arts.

Mention should be made of a third group of Hindu sects, along with Brahmanism and Buddhism, that is, Jainism. Jainism is traceable to the sixth century B.C. and was closely allied to the other two, especially to Buddhism. Members of this priestly sect believed in a separate existence of the soul after death, even the souls of animals. The only way for the soul to reach a perfect state was to suppress the body by means of abstinence, continence, and silence. They worshiped a group of seventy-two saints called Jains, twenty-four in each of the three ages of past, present, and future. The twenty-four of the early period were known also as teachers or prophets and called Tinthankaros. Each one has a name, and the one illustrated here is called Rsabhanatha, or the golden bull.

The followers of Jainism are divided into two very definite sects: the Digambaras and the Swetambaras, both naturally dedicated to the search for salvation. However, the Swetambaras, who wore white robes, believed that wearing clothes was not an impediment to achieving salvation, and they did admit women into their sect. The Digambaras, on the other hand, rejected all clothing as harmful to spiritual life and denied that women could ever attain salvation, Nirvana. To them, clothes were worldly possessions and their use made it impossible to attain Nirvana. Therefore they believed in nudity. Yet in all of Indian art, while there are many erotic sculptures of copulation, the number of nude young male figures is very limited, as is also the case with Chinese and Japanese art.

The examples of the young male in Indian art included in this book, therefore, are mainly figures of Buddha and his young followers or teachers known as bodhisattvas, or representations of the Brahman Siva. The passing of the Gupta period saw the beginning of the classic age with its resurgence of Brahamanism, during which hundreds of bronze statues were created, many showing Siva as Nataraja, or Lord of the Dance. He is typically shown with one foot on a dwarf and gesticulating with four hands. In one hand is a drum, symbolizing the recall to life of the powers of nature. In another is fire, which is to consume this rebirth and return it to its original repose. Life is created; life is destroyed, but not for the sake of annihilation, but always for the betterment of the soul. The aim of all life was to attain wisdom, or be with God.

Meanwhile Buddhism spread east to Indochina, China, and Japan. Here as in India, sculpture was represented by statues of Buddha and his bodhisattvas. However, to the austere, beautifully smooth bodies of these figures, the Chinese added their own concepts of decorativeness.

In painting, however, Chinese and Japanese art was quite unlike that of India. Indian painting is best known for its Persian miniatures. After the Gupta period, India was invaded by the Tartars who ruled the country as the Rajputs and whose art was religious and traditional. From 1000 to 1526 the Muhammadans overran India and set up the fabulous Mogul Empire, which lasted until the establishment of British rule in 1818. The famous Moguls, Akbar and his descendants, were enlightened rulers and lovers of the arts. It was his grandson, Shah Jahan, who built the fabulous Taj Mahal. This Persian art was secular in nature, and in its portrayal of the human form pictured mainly court life about the palace.

While the figures were painted flat and not in the round, they possessed a charming, delicate refinement. These Persian painters are best remembered for their enchanting illustrations for books, and many young males were the central subjects in their works.

Chinese and Japanese artists, on the other hand, almost ignored the young male. Their art was concerned with depicting trees, flowers, and birds. When they did paint the human form it was usually of old men and matriarchs, or fantastically grimacing actors. Only occasionally did they draw or paint a young boy.

While a great deal is known about Indian and the Oriental arts, comparatively little is yet known about the so-called primitive arts of Africa. However, African and Oceanian art today enjoy an enormous popularity. At first, at the end of the last century, they were studied as part of the ethnological aspect of life in these localities; now they are accepted as true works of art of another culture. Especially interest has centered on African and Oceanian sculpture. Until recently such primitive sculpture had been criticized on religious (its pagan concept) and moral grounds (its exaggerated size of the penis, although this is indicative of fertility worship). However, when early in this century art interest turned to the exotic, especially with the Fauvists, African and other primitive sculpture began to come into its own. Picasso and Matisse were greatly excited by this African art, and because of their espousal of it interest spread rapidly throughout the esthetic world.

Primitive sculptures themselves do not represent individuals, but types. They are full of the vitality of living. Thus these works are stylized not naturalistic. Individual works, as those shown here, do not have a wealth of art history behind them. They are presented here with just the basic facts of their origin, and the viewer is left to his own interpretive devices and intuition as to their basic meanings.

INDIAN
Fifth century
Buddha
Stone statue from Sarnath
Indian Museum, Calcutta

Coincident with the beginnings of the Christian era, this type of Buddha came into existence. He is a very human-looking god, but the absence of muscles and the ethereal smoothness of the body lift it above mortal beings.

INDIAN
Early fifth century
Standing Buddha
From Bengal
Copper, ht. 7 ft., 6 in.
City Museum and Art Gallery
Birmingham, England

This colossal, nearly one-ton figure of
Buddha from Sultanganj was cast in two
layers. Inside is a cylinder-like core,
which is overlayed on the outside with
copper. It is a Gupta-type figure, noted
for its precisely defined features, elaborate
curly hair, and lithe body, a real
embodiment of physical and spiritual
beauty.

INDIAN
Early sixth century
The Sanchi Torso
Stone sculpture
Victoria and Albert Museum
London

This brilliant Gupta-style sculpture is
perhaps the finest example of Indian
stone carving in existence. The torso
belonged to the figure of the Bodhisattva
Maitreya, a future Buddha who enjoyed
the following of a wide Buddhist cult
about the fifth and sixth centuries. It is
from Sanchi, a sacred site of Buddhism
in central India.

INDIAN
Eleventh to thirteenth century
Tīrthankaras Rsabhanātha
Museum Rietberg, Zurich

There is a stiffness and austerity to this
Jain image due to the abstract rendering
of the unadorned body. No muscles
show in this smooth nude. The entire
concept is one of spiritual perfection, in
which the body is shorn of any
imperfections or manifestations of worldly
existence. This particular Tīrthankaras is
always standing. He is reported to have
lived 8,400,000 years and to have been
500 poles high! The tiny figure of the
bull resting in what might be considered
a name plaque tells who the figure is:
Rsabhanātha means Lord Bull.

INDIAN
Twelfth century
Siva Natarājā, Lord of Chidambaram
Bronze
Museum Rietberg, Zurich
Collection v.d. Heydt, Hans Finsler photo

Siva, the third god in the Hindu trinity,
was known as the heavenly dancer. In
the form of Natarājā he is shown here
as Lord of the Dance. The Hindu religion
visualized its gods as idealized images
of man. Siva was considered as the most
generous of the gods.

185

INDIAN
Thirteenth century
Chola period
from Tanjore
Krishna as the Butter Thief
Bronze, ht. 19 in.
William Rockhill Nelson Gallery of Art
Kansas City, Missouri, Nelson Fund

This is one of the great and best-known
Indian sculptures relating to the Krishna
legend. The young boy brazenly raises
his right leg, and with a balancing arm
outstretched mischievously dances away
with the butter he has just stolen.
Krishna is an incarnation of the Brahman
god Vishnu.

CHINESE
T'ang Dynasty
Buddhist Monk
Stone, ht. c. 69 in.
including stone dowel
The Metropolitan Museum of Art
New York
Gift of A. W. Bahr, 1952

CHINESE
Sixth century
Wei(?) Dynasty
Figure of a Buddhist Priest
Bronze statuette
The Metropolitan Museum of Art
New York
Rogers Fund, 1928

INDIAN
Sixteenth century
Śiva as Naṭarājā
Museum of Fine Arts, Boston

CHINESE OR TIBETAN (LAMAIST)
Seventeenth century
Figure of Arhat. Bronze gilt, ht. 13½ in., base 9 × 6¼ in.
The Metropolitan Museum of Art, New York, Seymour Fund, 1952

RIZA-I-ABBASI
Early seventeenth century
Persian artist
Isfahan school
Kneeling Youth with Wine Cup
Line drawing
Ink, color, gold, 5½ × 3⅝ in.
Freer Gallery of Art, Washington, D.C.

This drawing is typical of the school of miniature paintings during the reign of the Shah Safi (1629–1642), which depicted court life of the Mogul emperors. This artist was one of the greatest in Persian history. The effeminate youth shown here represents a pourer of wine in a local tavern, where his youth and beauty were deliberately displayed to arouse the sexual passions of the patrons.

PERSIAN
Middle of sixteenth century
A Prince on Horseback
Brush drawing
*The Metropolitan Museum of Art
New York
George D. Pratt Bequest, 1945*

A delicate drawing that is of the same Safavid period as *Kneeling Youth with Wine Cup* and has the same feeling of dainty elegance.

JAPANESE
Late seventeenth century
Early Ukiyo-e school
A Boy with a Fan
Paper panel in gold and ink
49⁷/₁₆ × 20¹³/₁₆ in.
Freer Gallery of Art, Washington, D.C.

This young man could well have been
an actor. He is exquisitely portrayed in
a decorative costume and holds a
magnificently ornate fan. His expression
is one of confidence and intellect.

HOKUSAI, KATSUSHIKA
1760–1849, Japanese
Boy with a Flute
Late Edo period, Ukiyo-e school
Ink on paper, 4¹/₂ × 6¹/₄ in.
Freer Gallery of Art, Washington, D.C.

Of all the Japanese artists known to
Western culture, Hokusai is perhaps the
most popular. Adherents of the Ukiyo-e
school drew everyday, urban scenes.
Here the artist adds his own sensitive
touch to a sketch of a young boy to
whom, with a few simple dabs for eyes
and an endearing round face, he has
given a completely captivating
personality.

190

MEXICAN
Huaxtec culture
Tenth to fifteenth centuries
Adolescent Boy
Sandstone, ht. 4 ft., 7½ in.
Museo Nacional de Anthropologia
Mexico City

The Huaxtecs lived west of the Gulf
port of Tampico and occupied the land
of northern Veracruz and bordering
states. The height of their art was reached
in their stone sculptures of lifelike
figures. Perhaps the most famous example
extant is this *Adolescent Boy* from
Tamuin, San Luis Potosí. While it looks
very realistic, it is really closer to the
stark formality of ancient Egyptian
figures. This naked boy's body is covered
with tattoos resembling Huaxtec shell
carvings. He might have been a young
priest to the god Quetzalcoatl.

MEXICAN
300–1250
"El Pensador" Effigy
Pottery jar, ht. 8⅝ in.
Museum of the American Indian
Heye Foundation, New York

This contemplating figure of a young
male is a fine example of the pottery
art of western Mexico, Buena Vista site,
Colima. Such pre-Columbian art, with
its flowing contours, could easily have
exerted an influence on the classic
bronzes of modern sculptors such as
Rodin.

JUDAEAN
Eighth century B.C.
Horse and Rider
Pottery figurine
The Israel Museum, Jerusalem
Reifenberg Collection

The origin of this figure is incomplete except that it is known to be from the period of the Judaean Monarchy and probably comes from the region of the Judaean Hills (Hebron). It is interesting to note that the modern sculpture of Marino, also entitled *Horse and Rider,* bears a striking resemblance to this ancient work.

MEXICAN
Aztec
Xipe Totec
Clay, paint, ht. 56¾ in.
From Puebla
The Museum of Primitive Art
New York
Charles Uht photo

AFRICAN
Congo (Kinshasa), Mbole
Standing Male Figure
Wood, paint, ht. 33 in.
The Museum of Primitive Art, New York
Charles Uht photo

AFRICAN
Ivory Coast, Baule
Standing Male Figure
Wood, paint, ivory
Ht. 16⅝ in.
The Museum of Primitive Art, New York
Charles Uht photo

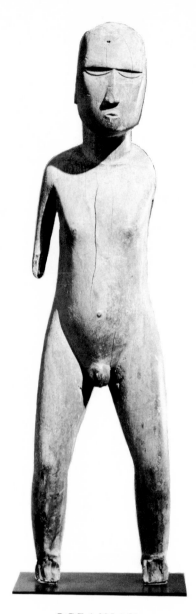

NEW GUINEA
Northeast
Middle Sepik River, Iatmul
Debating Stool
Wood, shell, paint, ht. 31 in.
The Museum of Primitive Art, New York
Charles Uht photo

NEW GUINEA
Northeast
Awatib village
Middle Sepik region
Ceremonial Stool
Blackened wood
Eyes inlaid with small shell-discs
Ht. 32¼ in.
Museum Voor Land- En Volkenkunde
(MLV 31847)
Rotterdam, Holland

OCEANIAN
Polynesia
Gambier Islands, Mangareva
Standing Male Figure
Wood, ht. 38¾ in.
The Museum of Primitive Art
New York
Charles Uht photo

194

AFRICAN
Twentieth century
Gabon, Fang tribe
Mortuary Figure
Wood, ht. 23 in.
The Brooklyn Museum
Brooklyn, New York

AFRICAN
Nigeria, Yoruba
Twin Figures
Wood, hts. 11⅛ in. and 11½ in.
The Museum of Primitive Art
New York
Charles Uht photo

KIRCHNER, ERNST LUDWIG, 1880–1938, German
Artillerymen (Soldiers in a Shower Room)
1915. Oil on canvas, 55¼ × 59⅜ in.
The Museum of Modern Art, New York
Gift of Mr. and Mrs. Morton D. May

A leading figure in *Die Brücke,* organized in 1905, this German
Expressionist made outdoor studies of the nude during the summer
months but then painted them symbolically rather than as his eye saw
them. Kirchner had just been inducted into the Army when he painted
this startling shower-room scene, which expresses his bitter condemnation
of military life and the severe physical and mental depressions it caused
him. Such erotic paintings as this one so angered Hitler that he ordered
Kirchner's paintings burned.

PART VI

In the Twentieth Century

Artwise, the twentieth century roared in like a pack of wild beasts. In fact, that was exactly what the early century's chief art movement was called, Fauvism, meaning wild beasts. It was initiated by Henri Matisse, and, while it lasted only for a brief period, it made a tremendous impact on paintings of that period. These painters were called wild beasts because of the way they distorted their shapes and the wild way they splashed vivid colors on their canvases. At this particular time African sculpture had been "discovered" and was very much in vogue. The Fauvists were greatly influenced by its primitiveness, simplicity of form, and fullness of living vitality. This group had their most famous exhibit at the Paris Salon in 1905. In Russia, Kruzma Petrov-Vodkin was following in the footsteps of Matisse.

At about the same time a completely opposite art movement was being initiated in Dresden, Germany, where a group of artists known as *Die Brücke* (The Bridge) were meeting, literally to express their feelings. They were the founders of German Expressionism, a movement which sought to express on canvas and in sculpture the inner feelings of mankind rather than outward appearances as seen by the eye. To understand their revolt against reality, it is necessary to take a look at the world at the early part of the twentieth century, especially before and after World War I. It was a time of uncertainty, of disillusionment, of emotional instability, of self-doubting, of psychotic fear in a world worried about its own destiny, especially in Germany, where a disastrous war had just been lost.

Another factor that materially affected the early twentieth-century artist was the decline of private art patronage due to, among other factors, the advancing machine age and the restrictions imposed on the accumulation of great wealth such as was the custom in the days of royal sovereigns. No longer did a patron order an artist to produce a specific work for him. The result was that the artist was forced to sell his work in the open market. Also he had to produce it before he could sell it, and the market value of what he produced was dependent upon the publicity he was accorded by the art critics of his day, who were for the most part conservative. The artist, therefore, not being able to make a living in the usual production channels of a capitalist society, was isolated into a world of his own. Thus his economic instability colored his viewpoint of life, beset him with loneliness and self-doubt, and fostered in him a violent emotional reaction to the society in which he lived. It was just such a psychological frame of mind that he tried to express in his works. It was not a pleasant world he was looking at, but one that to him was completely distorted. It is this distortion that best characterizes almost all modern art.

Thus the stage was tragically set for the spread of Expressionism, the most powerful art movement of the twentieth century. In 1909 another Expressionist group was formed in Munich, known as *Der Blaue Reiter* (The Blue Rider), whose members went even further in distorting forms and colors in order to convey their individual, inner, psychological understanding of life. Perhaps the greatest exponent of German Expressionism was Ernst Ludwig Kirchner, just one of many artists of this movement, who finally took his own life as a way out of his despondency. Others included Amedeo Modigliani, Chaim Soutine, and Wilhelm Lehmbruck. During the Nazi period in Germany, Hitler was so angered by the art of the Expressionists that he outlawed it and destroyed many hundreds of their works. Possibly he saw too close a resemblance between his own movement and theirs, with a mutual stress on morbidity, brutality, and corruption.

Not all forms of Expressionism were of such a negative quality. Many of the late nineteenth- and early twentieth-century artists turned from painting reality to attempting to express inner emotions, but did so without such bitterness. Cézanne was certainly an early Expressionist. So were Van Gogh, Gauguin, and James Ensor. Many sculptors were also influenced by the Expressionist movement, including Renée Sintenis and Gerhard Marcks.

The greatest single name in twentieth-century art is that of Pablo Picasso, whose earlier works only are included in this book, for the reason that they most admirably deal with the young male. On arriving in Paris from his native Spain, he began by working with the Fauvists, but soon developed many styles and techniques of his own. It is the Circus period of 1905 which is included here. These circus people he knew well, and in his canvases he treated them romantically and sensitively, expressing the deep, emotional tenderness he himself felt for humanity at that struggling period of his career. However, from 1906 to 1908 he reacted against these emotional subjects and founded an entirely new concept of painting called Cubism, in which he represented nature and figures in the form of cylinders, spheres, and cones. With Cubism he established a new art movement that was to attract many twentieth-century artists, both painters and sculptors, including such names as Jacques Lipchitz and Fernand Léger.

In the United States American artists were also turning away from the beautiful and were depicting the more sordid aspects of daily living and the commonplace as opposed to the romantic. In fact, so successful were they in transferring the drabness of life and locality to canvas that they were dubbed the Ashcan school. One of their leaders was Robert Henri, who did away entirely with initial drawing in favor of direct painting in an Impressionist style. George Bellows also belonged to this group. The big chance for progressive young artists to show their works came in 1913 with the now historically famous Armory Show in New York, which, not surprisingly, shocked an art public completely unprepared for what it saw.

As the century wore on many new and divergent art movements sprang up but were of such a nature that to distinguish a young male in any of their works would be extremely difficult. There were a few exceptions, of course. The young male is recognizable in the primitivism of Henri Rousseau, in the constructivism of Vladimir Tatlin, even in some of the surrealism of Salvador Dali. With the advent of Abstraction in 1935 artists turned to nonobjective painting. From Europe Abstraction was brought to the United States by Piet Mondrian, where it immediately gained a firm foothold. Since the Abstractionist did away with figure representation entirely, it is obvious the young male in art ceased to exist.

If the nineteenth century was comparatively devoid of great innovations in the field of sculpture, with the exception of the works of Rodin and Hildebrand, the twentieth century became a sculptor's paradise. At its beginning sculpture adhered to the traditional concepts of classical figures of a somewhat effete nature. But this soon changed. Just as painters revolted against traditional concepts, so sculptors developed new approaches to working in their media. For one thing, they began to see the importance of the material itself, from which they were creating their works. Whether it was stone, metal, wood, or plastic, they discovered that these materials possessed personalities of their own. Thus, instead of thinking in terms of carving a specific figure, the modern sculptor approached his medium with the idea of developing it into that figure. In other words, the texture, the grain, the monumental qualities, the finish were all integral parts of the final work. The work evolved out of the material.

Just as Expressionism changed the entire face of painting, so it changed the approach to sculpture. No longer was the classic representation of the human form, with its faithfulness to reality, enough. It was now necessary to reflect the artist's inner feelings in the completed work, to use related masses and open space, light and shade, rhythmic planes, slopes and surfaces to achieve expressiveness. Hollowed-out spaces were no longer voids but definite forms and part of the sculpture itself. Many of the new sculptors took their cues from Rodin but added their own modern innovations. First and foremost of the twentieth-century sculptors was Aristide Maillol, who introduced absolute freedom and simplicity of style, while stressing the volume and structure of the human form. His was a massive, quiet art, reflecting the post-Impressionist school. Georg Kolbe also followed in the manner of Rodin, but his figures were less realistic and more sensuously seductive. More extreme in their forms of Expressionism were Wilhelm Lehmbruck, Ernesto de Fiore, Gaston Lachaise, and Henry Moore. Moore expresses his emotions in his own individual freedom to handle his materials. More than any other modern sculptor he shapes the stone into a figure leaving the natural essentials of the material itself to create the figure. If the result was an identifiable image, fine, but it was not intentional. It could just as easily have ended up an abstract figure, as in the case of his renowned warrior.

Some modern sculptors were influenced by Cubism, as we mentioned in the case of Jacques Lipchitz. Other such sculptors include Raymond Duchamp-Villon and Ossip Zadkine, although they added a semiabstraction to their works. Other modern sculptors, surprisingly traditional in an art world so full of change, carved their young males with an eye for intrinsic beauty. Included in this category are R. Tait McKenzie, Hermon A. MacNeil, and Attilio Piccirilli. The 1940s saw serious abstract but still representational works of an exceedingly modern feeling in the creations of two Italians, Giacomo Manzù and Marino Marini. It was only with the advent of complete Abstraction that the young male in sculpture ceased to exist.

199

MATISSE, HENRI ÉMILE
1869–1954, French
Boy with Butterfly Net
1907. Oil on canvas, 69½ × 45 in.
The Minneapolis Institute of Arts
Minneapolis, Minnesota
John R. Van Derlip Fund

This life-size portrait of Allen Stein is
by one of the most famous leaders of
twentieth-century art. Characteristically
Fauve in style, the colors are exaggerated
and in greater variety than could ever be
found in nature.

SOROLLA Y BASTIDA, JOAQUÍN, 1863–1923, Spanish
Swimmers, 1905. Oil on canvas, 54¾ × 85½ in.
The Metropolitan Museum of Art, New York, Wolfe Fund, 1909

A thoroughly national painter, Sorolla stuck absolutely to realism and painted with bold simplicity and directness. He favored scenes that radiated joy, sunshine, and youthfulness. One of his favorite subjects was naked boys at the beach. In this one, called *Nadadores*, the swimming boys are totally surrounded by water, whereas most of his *playa* subjects included portions of the beach.

opposite:
HODLER, FERDINAND, 1853–1918, Swiss. *The Admired Youth*
C. 1903. Canvas, 82¾ × 117 in. *Kunsthaus, Zurich*

An early member of the German Expressionist movement, Hodler painted works of social significance. Here he symbolizes the unity of man in the repeated rhythm of the hand-holding women leaning toward a very effeminate nude male, who holds a stemmed flower in each hand in the Art Nouveau manner.

201

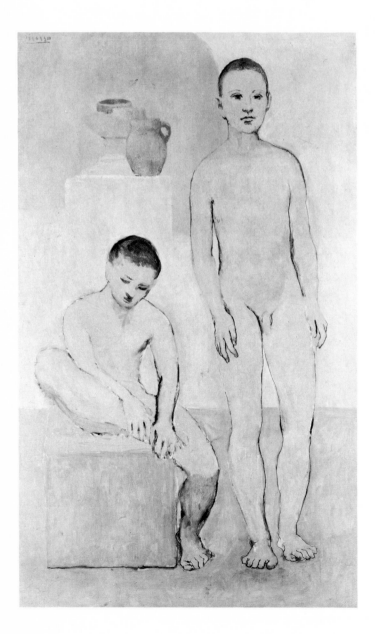

PICASSO, PABLO, 1881—
Spanish
Juggler with Still Life
1905. Cardboard, 39¼ × 27½ in.
Two Youths, 1905
Canvas, 59⅝ × 36⅞ in.
Both in the National Gallery of Art
Washington, D.C.
Chester Dale Collection

These paintings belong to Picasso's circus period. Himself a struggling young artist in Paris, he and his lovely Fernande were befriended by the harlequins and jugglers of the nearby Cirque Medrano, and they and their families became the models for his paintings of this period. He was expecially taken with the lonely, forlorn, and physically fragile young circus boys. These two works catch the affection he felt for such graceful adolescents with their appealingly androgynous bodies.

PICASSO. *Nude Boy*, 1905. Gouache and oil, 26¾ × 20½ in.
Hermitage Museum, Leningrad

Another example of Picasso's circus period, this naked youngster is in
the classical Hellenistic style.

LÉGER, FERNAND, 1881–1955, French. *Soldiers Playing Cards*, 1917
Oil on canvas, 50¾ × 76 in. *Kröller-Müller Museum, Otterlo, Holland*

A major force in the Cubist movement, Léger combined boldly colored
mechanical forms with human figures. This painting was based on
sketches the artist drew on active military duty in the trenches. The
figures are, ironically, robots that are completely defenseless against
the destructive will of the machine. Here they relax by playing cards
until, robot-like, they must unwillingly go into battle.

WEIE, EDVARD
1879–1943, Danish
Portrait of a Boy
C. 1920. Oil
*Statens Museum for Kunst
Copenhagen*

Although this Danish painter began his
career with traditional and naturalistic
paintings, he soon came under the
influence of the modern French school
of Matisse and Fauvism, as well as that
of Cézanne. In this colorful, sensitive
portrait, regarded as one of the artist's
best works, he combines a romantic
mood with superb brush and color
techniques.

204

MODIGLIANI, AMEDEO
1884–1920, Italian
Boy in Blue Jacket
1918
Oil on canvas, 36½ × 24¼ in.
*The Solomon R. Guggenheim Museum
New York*

The emotional distortions and fantastic
derangements of Modigliani's portraits
are a direct reflection and expression of
his own neurotic life, which ended before
his thirty-sixth birthday as a result of
alcohol and drugs. His elongated forms
bear a remarkable affinity to primitive
African sculpture. This young boy, like
Modigliani himself, sits in silent distress,
his empty, staring eyes expressing
acceptance of his own destiny, and
death.

SOUTINE, CHAIM
1894–1943, Russian-French
Portrait of a Boy
National Gallery of Art, Washington, D.C.
Chester Dale Collection

Another of the so-called *peintres maudits,*
or painters under a curse, along with
Modigliani, Gauguin, and Van Gogh,
Soutine was obsessed with death and
self-destruction. Thus his art expressed
his own anxieties, hates, and self-
recriminations, which took the form of
distorted shapes in vivid colors. Yet he
became a success before he was thirty-
five with his still lifes of beef carcasses,
dead fish, and plucked poultry. From
these he turned to painting menial youths
in the uniforms of their jobs. This
homely, loose-jointed boy with the
twisted nose and dated dress was
probably a busboy in a fashionable
French restaurant.

TATLIN, VLADIMIR
1885–1956, Russian
The Sailor, 1911–1912
Oil on canvas, 28⅛ × 28⅛ in.
Russian Museum, Leningrad

At the age of eighteen Tatlin, to escape
an unhappy childhood, became a sailor
on a ship bound for Egypt. This early
painting could have been a self-portrait
inspired by his seagoing experiences, for
he worked at sea until 1915. His style
was avant-garde and influenced by
Cézanne, Cubism, and other Abstract
techniques.

BUFFET, BERNARD
1928—, French
Self-Portrait, 1948
Oil on canvas, 82¼ × 40⅝ in.
*The Museum of Modern Art
New York*

Buffet's nudes, thin and emaciated,
convey the artist's belief that the world
is tragic and without hope. He is a
painter with a social conscience, who
portrays human misery, and never more
starkly than in this rendering of himself
at the age of twenty in a bare, virtually
unfurnished flat.

PETROV-VODKIN, KRUZMA, 1878–1939, Russian
The Playing Boys, 1911
Oil on canvas. *Russian Museum, Leningrad*

Impressed by primitive art and the works of Matisse, this artist painted
in strong blues and greens. Against such a background he starkly
portrays the nude figures of two boys. One of the chief appeals of this
painting is its fluid rhythm and mystical quality. This was one of
Petrov-Vodkin's early works.

BECKMANN, MAX
1884–1950, German
Rugby-Spieler, 1929
Oil, 82¾ × 29¼ in.
Stadtisches Kunstmuseum, Duisburg

One of the most powerful of the German
Expressionists of the first quarter of this
century, Beckmann later joined a group
called the "New Objectivity." As can
be seen by this painting of bold,
strikingly drawn ballplayers grouped
closely together, this new trend in style
was characterized by a harsh yet magic
realism. The crazily mixed-up figures are
symbolic of the painter's view of an
upside-down world.

SCHARFF, WILLIAM
1886–1959, Danish
Boys Looking at a Toad
1941. 76 × 52⅜ in.
Statens Museum for Kunst, Copenhagen

This outstanding young modernist, who
was greatly influenced by Cézanne, was
much on exhibit in Copenhagen around
1918. In his later works, as in this scene,
he painted mainly the human form.

VIGELAND, GUSTAV, 1869–1943, Norwegian
Monument to Beethoven, 1906. ht. 60¼ in.
Vigeland Museet, Oslo, K. Teigen photo

Norway's best-known sculptor designed several monuments to famous people shortly after working on the Trondheim Cathedral statuary. This Beethoven is one of them. Following its creation Vigeland spent most of the rest of his working life on pieces for Sculpture Park outside of Oslo.

LEHMBRUCK, WILHELM
1881-1919, German
Standing Youth, 1913
Cast stone, ht. 7 ft., 8 in.
The Museum of Modern Art, New York
Gift of Abby Aldrich Rockefeller

Influenced by German Gothic and Art
Nouveau, Lehmbruck used excessive
elongations in his sculptures to express
his own hypersensitivity and worry over
the state of the world in the World
War I years. The boy's thin body rises
straight up, and the frown on his face
expresses the artist's own disapproval
of the world around him. This outlook
along with poor health finally drove him
to suicide.

opposite:
LEHMBRUCK
Prodigal Son, c. 1912
Drypoint, $11^5/_8 \times 7^7/_8$ in.
Fogg Art Museum
Harvard University
Cambridge, Massachusetts
Gray Collection

Of the many melancholy drawings left
by Lehmbruck, this is one of the most
touching, sensitive, and sensuous. The
repentant boy's head, buried in his own
shoulder, is resting in his father's arms.
The mood is one of complete forgiveness.
With these two nudes Lehmbruck again
shows his dedication to the beauty of the
human form.

211

MAILLOL, ARISTIDE
1861–1944, French
Young Cyclist, 1907
Bronze, ht. 38 in.
Fogg Art Museum, Harvard University
Cambridge, Massachusetts

It was not until he reached the age of
forty that Maillol turned to sculpture,
whereupon he became the leading
sculptor of his day. The classical serenity
of this masterpiece was patterned on
Greek works. Among this artist's statues
the male nude was unusual as he
preferred carving mature females.

FIORE, ERNESTO DE
1884–1945, Italian-German
The Soldier, 1918
Bronze, ht. 50⅜ in.
Kunsthalle, Hamburg

Fiore followed very much the style of Maillol and Adolf Hildebrand, stressing pictorial qualities. Others in this same group included Lehmbruck, Sintenis, Kolbe, and Marcks. While Fiore was born in Rome, he became a German citizen in 1914, then moved to Brazil in 1936.

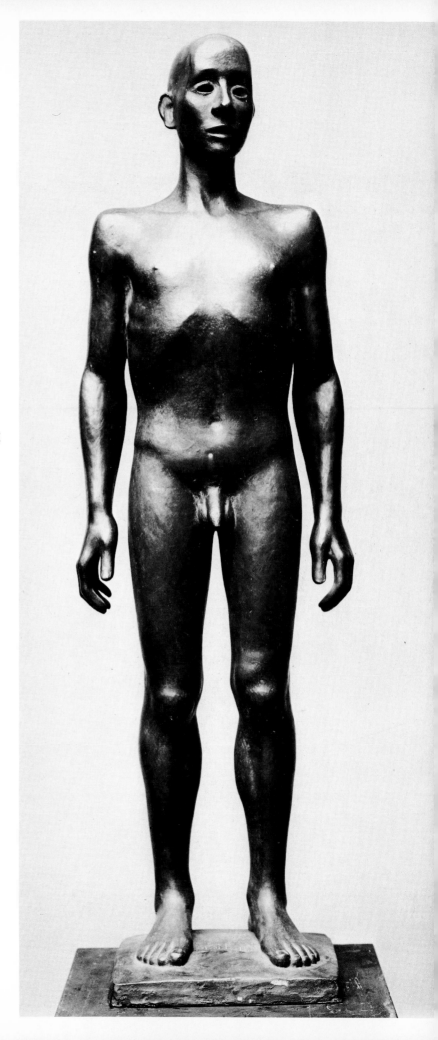

SINTENIS, RENÉE
1888–1965, German
Football Player
1927. Bronze, ht. 16 in.
Kröller-Müller Museum
Otterlo, Holland

This sculptress loved to portray action
in her works, which were a blend of
Impressionism and Expressionism. When
she carved a foal it was either kicking
up its heels or frolicking. One of her
pieces was Paavo Nurmi running,
another a boxer, another a polo player.
In this remarkably dynamic statue of a
football player, he appears to have just
kicked the ball with all his might.

DUCHAMP-VILLON, RAYMOND
1876–1918, French
Torso of a Young Athlete
1910. Bronze, ht. 21⅝ in.
Museum of Modern Art, Paris

Duchamp-Villon used traditional themes
in modern form. This striking athlete
could have come from ancient Greek
ruins, except that its energy, combined
with the simplicity and fullness of the
chest and shoulders, makes it a modern
masterpiece.

RICHIER, GERMAINE
1904–1959, French
Torso of a Youth
Bronze, ht. 43 in.
The Israel Museum, Jerusalem
The Billy Rose Art Garden

This sculptress was an assistant to
Bourdelle. Carving the human figure
was for her the best way to express her
own human experiences. She used
corroded surfaces in her works to
symbolize the decaying of all life matter.

ZADKINE, OSSIP
1890–1967, French
Torso Clementius
1941
Veined marble, ht. 38½ in.
Kröller-Müller Museum
Otterlo, Holland

Born in Smolensk, Russia, Zadkine
moved to France, where he came under
the influence of the works of Rodin and
of Cubism. Later he migrated to the
United States. Here he found a marble
sepulchral column on the grave of a
Negro named John Clement. He used it
to carve this torso.

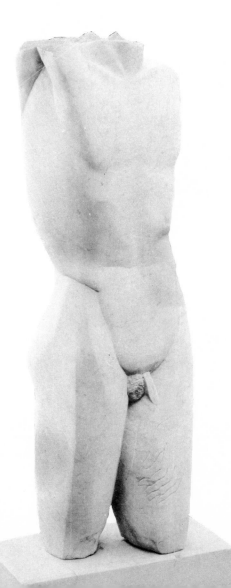

215

MARCKS, GERHARD, 1889—, German. *Friends,* 1934
Bronze. *Museum of Fine Arts, Boston*

Strongly influenced by Lehmbruck, Marcks used in his sculptures the
angular forms that so intrigued the German Expressionists. The two
youths in this statue show a deep psychological rapproachement to
each other.

MARCKS. *Prometheus II*, 1948. Bronze, ht. 30¾ in.
Busch-Reisinger Museum, Harvard University, Cambridge, Massachusetts
Keller of Belmont photo

The use of empty spaces gave Marcks's works a powerful three-dimensional scope and an impression of massiveness, even though this youth's warped body remains angular and slender.

KOLBE, GEORG, 1877–1947, German. *The Dancer*, 1914
Bronze, ht. 30 in. *Busch-Reisinger Museum, Harvard University*
Cambridge, Massachusetts. Anonymous gift in memory of Minnie S. Kuhn

Following closely the style of Maillol, Kolbe enjoyed working in bronze
and preferred to create nude figures, especially those in motion. This
dancer is almost leaping from the pedestal, as every part of his body is
engaged in movement.

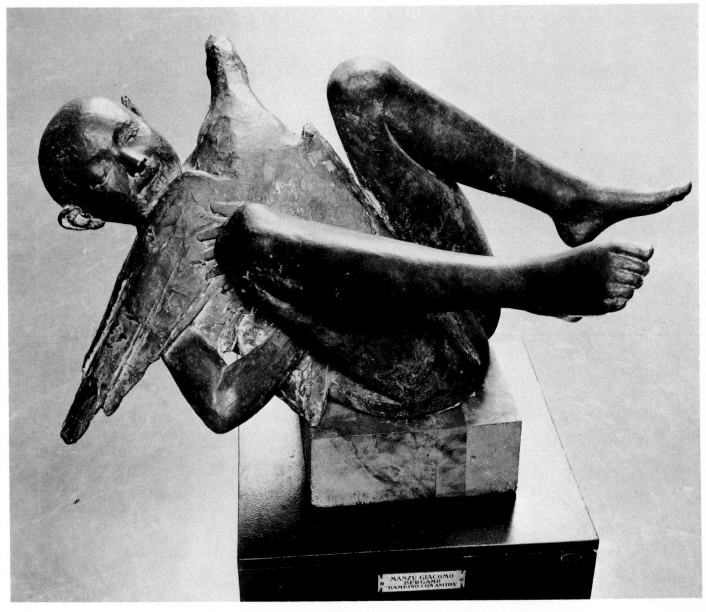

MANZÙ, GIACOMO, 1908—, Italian. *Boy with Goose,* 1947
Bronze, ht. 19⅝ in. *Civico Museo Revoltella, Trieste*

This sculptor is considered the leading Italian artist. In 1941 he was
appointed professor of sculpture at the Albertina Academy in Turin.
Shown in Milan at the 1947 Exhibition, this freely expressed work is
definitely classic and with the Renaissance influence of Donatello. The
juxtaposition of the two figures, the naked boy lying on his back with
his parted legs in the air and the bird with its spread wings, creates an
exceedingly dynamic image.

MILLES, CARL
1875–1955, Swedish
Figures from the Orpheus Fountain
Cranbrook Academy of Art
Bloomfield Hills, Michigan

This modern Scandinavian artist spent many years of his life in the United States. He left to posterity some of the most beautiful fountains in the world, not even surpassed by those of ancient Greece. He combined bronze and stone into beautifully executed rhythmic arrangements.

opposite:
MARINI, MARINO, 1901—, Italian. *Horse and Rider*, c. 1949
Bronze, 71 × 49 × 32 in. *Walker Art Center, Minneapolis, Minnesota*
Eric Sutherland photo

Archaic-style works of the Egyptian and Etruscan preclassical periods inspired this artist, whose sculptures are characterized by rough surfaces and shapeless forms. Marini's favorite theme, which he rendered in many paintings, drawings, and sculptures, was the horse and rider. In some, both horse and rider are leaning backward, in this sculpture both are upright. The startling result is one of abstract, primitive sensuality.

GIACOMETTI, ALBERTO
1901–1966, Swiss
Walking Man, 1960
Bronze, ht. 71¾ in.
*Museum of Art, Carnegie Institute
Pittsburgh, Pennsylvania*

A surrealist, Giacometti spent five
arduous years studying the human form.
The result of this study and of an
extended stay during 1938 in the hospital
was the emergence of his style of an
extremely elongated figure carved with
rough texture. This walking man is tall,
emaciated, with all flesh stripped from
his bony body.

KIRCHNER, ERNST LUDWIG
1880–1938, German
Two Friends, 1925–26
Larchwood painted with tempera, ht. 69 in.
Kunstsammlung, Basel

Emulating the simplicity of the medieval
craftsmen, this work is nevertheless a
meaningful and psychological probe into
the artist's own feelings and an excellent
example of German Expressionism.

TUOHY, PATRICK
1894–1930, Irish
A Mayo Peasant Boy
Oil on canvas, 31 × 21 in.
Municipal Gallery of Modern Art
Dublin, Barry Mason photo

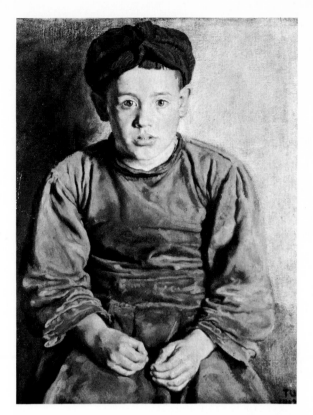

In many sections of Ireland the peasants have a custom of dressing boys and girls in the same costume. Thus dressed, this engaging lad possesses all the charm and lovableness of a typical Irish country youth. There is a certain similarity between this painting and the *Lamp Boy* of James Ensor.

MOORE, HENRY
1898—, English
Warrior with a Shield
1953–1954. Bronze, ht. 5 ft.
The Minneapolis Institute of Arts
Minneapolis, Minnesota

Sculpture belongs outdoors where the sunlight can bring it alive. This was the feeling Moore had in relation to his massive works, designed to stand out as part of the landscape. During his visit to Greece in 1950 he was impressed with the surviving pieces of the Archaic period. These he translated into modern idiom, as with this dynamic, dying warrior with his enigmatic head, shield outstretched, and sensuously seated body.

223

BELLOWS, GEORGE WESLEY
1882–1925, American
Forty-Two Kids
1907. Oil
The Corcoran Gallery of Art
Washington, D.C.

Because of his aggressive portrayal of
everyday American life, Bellows has
been considered *the* American artist. As
such, he was intensely interested in
masculine activities, especially sports
and recreation. What could be more
typical than this scene of a large group
of unassuming young boys swimming off
of a dilapidated city pier? Such scenes
characterized the Ashcan school of
painting.

224

TCHELITCHEW, PAVEL
1898–1957, Russian-American
The Whirlwind, 1939
Oil on canvas, 28½ × 23¾ in.
*The Metropolitan Museum of Art
New York
Arthur H. Hearn Fund, 1950*

This painting of a weird conglomeration
of wild youngsters illustrates an arbitrary
distortion of perspective.

TCHELITCHEW
Man and Child, 1935
Gouache watercolor and brown ink
20⅜ × 12¼ in.
*The Wadsworth Atheneum
Hartford, Connecticut
Lifar Collection*

Not only a painter, Tchelitchew was a
top designer of ballet costumes and
scenery, both of which he did for the
ballet *L'Errante,* as well as collaborating
on the book with George Balanchine. It
was performed in Paris in 1933. This
sketch is of one of the moments in the
ballet.

opposite:
KUHN, WALT. 1880–1949, American. *Young Clown,* 1932
Oil on canvas, 30 × 25 in. *The Denver Art Museum, Denver, Colorado*
Some artists become known for their repeated use of the same theme
or type of portraiture. Kuhn's most brilliant paintings were his simple
figures, particularly the circus performer. This youthful clown wears
an expression of disarming honesty and questioning perplexity.

KARFIOL, BERNARD, 1886–1952, American. *Boys and Ponies,* 1927
Oil on canvas, 36 × 27¼ in.
Whitney Museum of American Art, New York

Influenced by the Impressionism of Renoir and Cézanne and the manner
in which they painted male nudes, Karfiol added his own intense feeling
of tenderness to his renderings of young males. Toward the young nude
figure his approach was pagan, intimate, and spontaneous.

KARFIOL
Boy Bathers, 1916
Oil on canvas, 28 × 36 in.
Whitney Museum of American Art
New York

With their unpretentious beauty of form
and activity, these young naked bathers
are comparable to Picasso's youths of
his circus period.

POOR, HENRY VARNUM
1888—, American
In Western Garb, 1937
Oil on masonite, 24 × 20 in.
Wichita Art Museum, Wichita, Kansas
The Roland P. Murdock Collection

In 1917 Poor moved to the West to
teach. Being an Easterner, he must have
thought Western clothes were strange and
amusing. Thus he painted this portrait
of, in his own words, "an eastern boy
gone 'western.'"

WYETH, ANDREW NEWELL
1917—, American
Albert's Son, 1959
Tempera, 29 × 24¼ in.
Nasjonal Galleriet, Oslo, Norway
O. Vaering photo

Undoubtedly America's most popular
modern painter today, Andrew Wyeth
in an age of Abstractism has stuck to
reality in his style and subject matter.
This eleven-year-old boy was leaning
against a barn door one day when the
artist saw him and painted him in this
rural setting.

PARK, DAVID, 1911–1960, American. *Four Men,* 1958
Oil on canvas, 57 × 92 in.
Whitney Museum of American Art, New York, Geoffrey Clements photo

This modern California painter switched from Abstractism to a
figurative style that was close to German Expressionism. The rigidity
of his figures in this painting heightens the intensity of effect in his
portrayal of these sepulchral, seminude bathers.

BURLIN, PAUL
1886—, American
Young Man Alone with His Face
1944. Oil on canvas, 39 × 32 in.
*Whitney Museum of American Art
New York*

An artist caught up in the American
dissent movement of the early part of
this century and a member of the Ashcan
school, Burlin exhibited four drawings
at the famous 1913 Armory Show in
New York. During the forties his
paintings became more daring, abstract,
and prone to grotesque and brutal
distortions. In this portrait the artist
combines tragedy, laughter, absurdity,
and a hideous hilarity—all intended to
convey the innate tragedy of the human
race.

JAMES, ALEXANDER ROBERTSON
1890–1946, American
Black Boy, 1935
Oil on wood, 16 × 12¾ in.
*The Metropolitan Museum of Art
New York, Arthur H. Hearn Fund, 1937*

It was quite logical that this son of
William James, the famous American
philosopher and psychologist, would
paint people realistically as they appeared
in informal real life. For this purpose he
soon retired to Dublin, New Hampshire,
so that he could paint rural subjects as
he wished. He excelled especially in his
bare-chested stalwart Negro portraits, as
in this powerful *Black Boy.*

CADMUS, PAUL, 1904—, American. *Two Boys on a Beach #1*
Engraving. *Private Collection, New York*

The works of this modern realist are effectively shocking. This bold
drawing is explicitly erotic and sexual with an obvious emotional
relationship between the two young men.

MC KENZIE, R. TAIT
1867–1938, American
The Competitor, 1906.
Bronze, one-half life size
*The Metropolitan Museum of Art
New York, Rogers Fund, 1909*

Of all modern sculptors McKenzie
concentrated most on using young
athletes as his subject matter. His models
were the youths who practiced their
physical fitness exercises on the Long
Island beaches by the sea.

230

LIPCHITZ, JACQUES
1891—, Lithuanian-American
Sailor with a Guitar, 1914
Bronze, ht. 30 in.
Philadelphia Museum of Art, Philadelphia

Influenced by Picasso's Cubism, Lipchitz
felt at the time that Cubism offered a
new way to represent nature and express
himself. This work was done in Madrid,
where the use of flat, overlapping planes
in sculptural pieces was in vogue. This
is a much more realistic figure than in
the later nonrepresentational works of
one of today's leading sculptors.

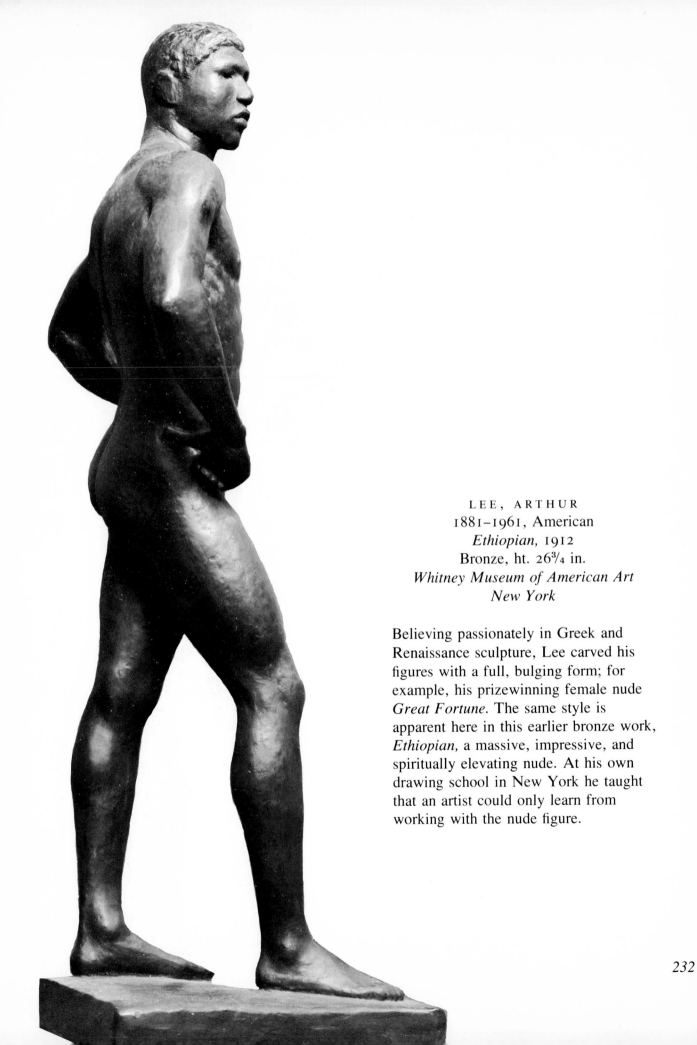

LEE, ARTHUR
1881–1961, American
Ethiopian, 1912
Bronze, ht. 26¾ in.
*Whitney Museum of American Art
New York*

Believing passionately in Greek and
Renaissance sculpture, Lee carved his
figures with a full, bulging form; for
example, his prizewinning female nude
Great Fortune. The same style is
apparent here in this earlier bronze work,
Ethiopian, a massive, impressive, and
spiritually elevating nude. At his own
drawing school in New York he taught
that an artist could only learn from
working with the nude figure.

FERGUSON, DUNCAN
1901—, American
Male Figure
Bronze, ht. 72 in.
Whitney Museum of American Art
New York
An excellent example of the modern
massive sculptural treatment in the
manner of Arthur Lee and Gaston
Lachaise.

233

PICCIRILLI, ATTILIO
1866–1945, Italian-American
Spirit of Youth, 1925
Carrara marble, ht. 12½ ft.
Virginia Military Institute
Lexington, Virginia

This Italian-born artist settled in the
United States in 1888 and soon began
receiving commissions for monuments
and figures, which he carved in the
smooth neoclassical style of the
nineteenth century. Inspiration for this
nude statue came from the artist's
infatuation with Michelangelo's *David*
and the bravery of young American
soldiers of World War I in the Battle
of Piave.

MACNEIL, HERMON A.
1866–1947, American
The Sun Vow, 1919. Bronze
The Metropolitan Museum of Art
New York, Rogers Fund, 1919

In the years around World War I there
was great interest in the United States
in traveling exhibits of small bronze
sculptures by top artists. These were
created imaginatively and independent of
art committee rules or regulations. This
MacNeil piece is on his favorite subject:
the American Indian posing in emotional
situations, such as his *The Coming of
the White Man* and this *The Sun Vow*.

BEN-SHMUEL, AHRON
1903—, American
Torso of a Boy, 1930
Black granite, ht. 28¾ in.
The Museum of Modern Art, New York

This artist learned his trade as a granite
cutter both in the United States and
Egypt, where he spent many years
alongside the native granite cutters and
at the same time studied Egyptian
sculpture. As a result of his working
with hard, massive granite, his
sculptures possess powerful volume, yet,
at the same time, he carves simplified
planes. *Torso of a Boy* is infused with
a dynamic strength of living and touched
with a feeling of repose.

ROX, HENRY
1899—, American. *Ritual,* 1942
Terra-cotta, ht. 16½ in.
Addison Gallery of American Art
Phillips Academy
Andover, Massachusetts

Modern, yet leaning heavily on the
Baroque style, Rox achieved his animated
effects and emotional impact by using
a sparcity of detail. He is more concerned
with relief than fullness. His works can
be viewed from any angle without sensing
any abrupt interruption. He was fond of
interpreting dreamy adolescents and
introverted youngsters.

LACHAISE, GASTON
1882–1935, American
Man Walking
1933. Bronze, 23¼ in.
*Whitney Museum of American Art
New York*

While Lachaise's absorption with the
nude male figure was less intense than
his interest in his massive females, this
full-length work is much more realistic
than most of his females. All of his
works were dedicated to normal, robust
beauty, with strong emphasis on the
sexual qualities of the human body.
Originally criticized as in bad taste, his
heroic sculptures are now acclaimed
everywhere.

opposite:
LACHAISE
Nude Male, c. 1934
Blue ink and pencil drawing
23⅝ × 18⅝ in.
The Lachaise Foundation

Lachaise rendered his drawings in stark
outline, as the boldness and imagination
characterizing this sketch of a young
male nude admirably shows. Perhaps all
of Lachaise's art was a rebellion against
conservatism and the puritanical
environment into which he was born in
Paris.

BIBLIOGRAPHY

APOLLONIO, UMBRO. *Marino Marini: Sculptor.* Milan: Edizioni del Milione, 1953.

ARNOLD, BRUCE. *A Concise History of Irish Art.* New York: Frederick A. Praeger, Inc., 1968.

Art Digest, The, October 15, 1930; January 15, 1937; October 1, 1938; August 1, 1947; November 1, 1947.

ART INSTITUTE OF CHICAGO, THE. *A Guide to the Paintings in the Permanent Collection.* Chicago, 1932.

Art News, December 15, 1945; May, 1951.

AYMAR, GORDON C. *The Art of Portrait Painting.* Philadelphia: Chilton Book Company, 1967.

BALLO, GUIDO. *Modern Italian Painting: from Futurism to the Present Day.* Translated by Barbara Wall. London: Thames and Hudson Ltd., 1958.

BARKER, VIRGIL. *American Painting: History and Interpretation.* New York: The Macmillan Company, 1950.

BARR, ALFRED H., JR. *Matisse: His Art and His Public.* New York: The Museum of Modern Art, 1951.

———. *Picasso: Fifty Years of His Art.* New York: The Museum of Modern Art, 1946.

BATTISTA, EUGENIO. *Velázquez.* Milan: Arti Grafiche Ricordi, 1964.

BAZIN, GERMAIN. *A History of Art from Prehistoric Times to the Present.* New York: Houghton Mifflin Company, 1959.

BEAN, JACOB, AND STAMPFLE, FELICE. *Drawings from New York Collections: The Italian Renaissance.* New York: The Metropolitan Museum of Art, 1965.

———. *The Seventeenth Century in Italy.* New York: The Metropolitan Museum of Art, 1967.

BERENSON, BERNARD. *Caravaggio: His Incongruity and His Fame.* London: Chapman & Hall, 1953.

———. *The Drawings of the Italian Painters.* Chicago: University of Chicago Press, 1938.

———. *The Italian Painters of the Renaissance.* London: The Phaidon Press Ltd., 1952.

BERGER, KLAUS. *Géricault and His Works.* Translated by Winslow Ames. Lawrence, Kansas: University of Kansas Press, 1955.

BERGER, RENÉ. *Discovery of Painting.* New York: The Viking Press, 1963.

BIRD, PAUL. *Fifty Paintings by Walt Kuhn.* New York: Studio Publications Incorporated, 1940.

BLACK, MARY, AND LIPMAN, JEAN. *American Folk Painting.* New York: Clarkson N. Potter, Inc., 1966.

BOLTON, THEODORE. "Henry Inman, An Account of His Life and Work." *Art Quarterly,* III, 1940.

BORGESE, LEONARDO. *Nineteenth Century Italian Painting.* Milan: Arti Grafiche Ricordi, 1964.

BOSTON MUSEUM OF FINE ARTS. *Catalogue of Paintings,* 1921.

BOSWELL, PEYTON, JR. *Varnum Poor.* New York: Harper & Brothers, 1941.

BREDIUS, A. (ed.). *The Paintings of Rembrandt.* Vienna: Phaidon-Verlag, 1936.

BREUNING, MARGARET. "Vital Sculpture," *Art Digest,* October 1, 1946.

BRION, MARCEL. *Michelangelo.* Translated by James Whitall. New York: The Greystone Press, 1940.

———. *Romantic Art.* New York: McGraw-Hill Book Company, Inc., 1960.

BROWN, MILTON W. *American Painting: from the Armory Show to the Depression.* Princeton, New Jersey: Princeton University Press, 1955.

BROWN, W. NORMAN. "The Gentle Jains," *Asia,* March, 1934.

CANADAY, JOHN. *Mainstreams of Modern Art.* New York: Holt, Rinehart & Winston, Inc., 1959.

CASKEY, LACEY D. *Catalogue of Greek and Roman Sculpture.* Boston: Museum of Fine Arts with Harvard University Press, Cambridge, 1925.

CASSON, JEAN; LANGIN, EMIL; AMD PEVSNER, NIKOLAUS. *Gateway to the Twentieth Century: Art and Culture in a Changing World.* New York: McGraw-Hill Book Company, Inc., 1962.

CASSON, STANLEY. *XXth Century Sculptors.* London: Oxford University Press, 1930.

CASTELFRANCO, GIORGIO. *Donatello.* New York: Reynal & Company, Inc., n.d.

CHASTEL, ANDRÉ. *The Age of Humanism: Europe 1480–1530.* New York: McGraw-Hill Book Company, Inc., 1963.

CHENEY, SHELDON. *A New World History of Art.* New York: Holt, Rinehart & Winston, Inc., 1956.

————. *A Primer of Modern Art.* New York: Tudor Publishing Company, 1945.

————. *The Story of Modern Art.* New York: The Viking Press, 1941.

CLAPP, FREDERICK MORTIMER. *Jacopo Carucci da Pontormo.* New Haven, Connecticut: Yale University Press, 1916.

CLARK, KENNETH. *The Nude: A Study in Ideal Form.* New York: Pantheon Books, 1956.

————. *Piero Della Francesca.* London: The Phaidon Press Ltd., 1951.

COOMARASWAMY, ANANDA K. *History of Indian and Indonesian Art.* New York: E. Weyhe, 1927.

COUNTRY BEAUTIFUL, EDITORS OF. *Great Art Treasures in America's Smaller Museums.* Waukesha, Wisconsin: Country Beautiful Foundation, Inc., 1967.

COURTHION, PIERRE, AND CAILLER, PIERRE (eds.). *Portrait of Manet by Himself and His Contemporaries.* Translated by Michael Ross. London: Cassell & Company Ltd., 1960.

COWDREY, BARTLETT, AND WILLIAMS, HERMANN WARNER, JR. *William Sidney Mount: 1807–1868, An American Painter.* New York: Columbia University Press, 1944.

CROSS, LOUISE. "Ahron Ben-Schmuel," *Arts Weekly,* November 26, 1932.

CRUTTWELL, MAUD. *Luca Signorelli.* London: George Bell and Sons, 1899.

DENIS, VALENTIN, AND DE VRIES, T. E. (eds.). *Picture History of World Art,* Vol. II. New York: Harry N. Abrams, Inc., n.d.

DETROIT INSTITUTE OF ARTS. *Bulletin,* Vol. XXIV, No. 1, 1944.

DIEHL, GASTON. *Modigliani.* New York: Crown Publishers, Inc., 1969.

DOCKSTADER, FREDERICK J. *Indian Art in Middle America.* New York: Graphic Society Publishers, Ltd., 1964.

Drawings from Old Masters. Third series. New York: Frederick A. Stokes Company, n.d.

DURANT, WILL. *The Renaissance: A History of Civilization in Italy from 1304–1576* A.D. New York: Simon and Schuster, Inc., 1953.

EGGENBERGER, DAVID (ed.). *Encyclopedia of World Art.* 15 vols. New York: McGraw-Hill Book Company, Inc., 1959–1968.

ELIOT, ALEXANDER. *Three Hundred Years of American Painting.* New York: Time Inc., 1957.

EMMERICH, ANDRÉ. *Art Before Columbus.* New York: Simon and Schuster, Inc., 1963.

FAISON, S. LANE, JR. *A Guide to the Art Museums of New England.* New York: Harcourt, Brace and Company, 1958.

FINEBERG, ALEXANDER J. *An Authentic Portrait of Robert Peake.* Oxford, England: Walpole Society, Vol. 9, 1921.

FIUMI, N. G. "The Portraits of Antonio Mancini," *Creative Art,* February, 1928.

FRÉDÉRIC, LOUIS. *The Art of India: Temples and Sculpture.* New York: Harry N. Abrams, Inc., 1959.

"Frederick Macmonnies, Sculpture," *Brush and Pencil,* April, 1902.

FREEDBERG, SIDNEY J. *Parmigianino: His Works in Painting.* Cambridge, Massachusetts: Harvard University Press, 1950.

FREEMAN, LUCY JANE. *Italian Sculpture of the Renaissance.* New York: The Macmillan Company, 1917.

FURTWÄNGLER, ADOLF. *Masterpieces of Greek Sculpture*. Chicago: Argonaut Publishers, Inc., 1964.

GARDNER, ALBERT TEN EYCK. *Winslow Homer, American Artist: His World and His Work*. New York: Bramhall House, 1961.

GAUNT, WILLIAM, AND ROE, F. GORDON. *Etty and the Nude*. Leigh-on-the-Sea, Essex, England: F. Lewis, Publishers, Limited, 1943.

GETLEIN, FRANK. *Art Treasures of the World*. New York: Clarkson N. Potter, Inc., 1968.

GIANNELLI, GIULIO (ed.). *The World of Ancient Rome*. London: Macdonald & Co., Ltd., 1967.

GIEDION-WELCKER, CAROLA. *Contemporary Sculpture: An Evolution in Volume and Space*. London: Faber and Faber, 1956.

GILMORE, MYRON P. *The World of Humanism: 1453–1517*. New York: Harper & Row, Publishers, 1952.

GODFREY, F. M. *Italian Sculpture 1250–1700*. London: Alec Tiranti Ltd., 1967.

GODWIN, BLAKE-MORE. *Catalogue of European Paintings*. Toledo, Ohio: The Toledo Museum of Art., n.d.

GOLDSCHEIDER, LUDWIG. *El Greco: Paintings, Drawings and Sculptures*. Third edition. London: Phaidon Publishers, Inc., 1954.

_____. *Five Hundred Self-Portraits*. Translated by J. Byam Shaw. Vienna: Phaidon Press, 1937.

GOLDWATER, ROBERT. *Paul Gauguin*. New York: Harry N. Abrams, Inc., 1928.

GOMBRICH, ERNST HANS. *The Story of Art*. London: The Phaidon Press Ltd., 1957.

GOODRICH, LLOYD. *Thomas Eakins: His Life and Work*. New York: Whitney Museum of American Art, 1933.

_____. *Winslow Homer*. New York: The Macmillan Company, 1944.

_____, AND BAER, JOHN I. H. *American Art of Our Century*. New York: Whitney Museum of American Art and Frederick A. Praeger, Inc., 1961.

GRABAR, ANDRÉ. *The Beginnings of Christian Art*. London: Thames and Hudson, Ltd., 1967.

GRAY, CAMILLA. *The Great Experiment: Russian Art 1863–1922*. New York: Harry N. Abrams, Inc., 1962.

GREEN, SAMUEL. *American Art: A Historical Survey*. New York: The Ronald Press, 1966.

GRIDLEY, MARION E. *American Indian Statues*. Chicago: The Amerindian, 1966.

GRIGSON, GEOFFREY. *English Drawing from Samuel Cooper to Given John*. London: Thames and Hudson, Ltd., 1955.

HAESAERTS, PAUL. *James Ensor*. New York: Harry N. Abrams, Inc., 1959.

HALE, PHILIP L. *Vermeer*. Boston: Hale, Cushman & Flint Incorporated, 1937.

HAMILTON, GEORGE HEARD. *Raymond Duchamp-Villon 1876–1918*. New York: Walker & Company, 1967.

HANDLER, GERHARD. *Deutsche Maler der Gegenwart*. Berlin: Rembrandt-Verlag GMBH, 1956.

HAUSENSTEIN, WILHELM. *Der Nackte Mensch in der Kunst Aller Zeiter und Völker*. Munich: R. Piper & Co., 1913.

HEILMEYER, ALEXANDER. *Adolf von Hildebrand*. Munich: Verlag von Albert Langen, 1922.

HEINRICH, THEODORE ALLEN. *Art Treasures in the Royal Ontario Museum*. Toronto: McClelland and Stewart Limited, 1963.

HENDY, PHILIP. *Catalogue of the Exhibited Paintings and Drawings: The Isabella Gardner Museum*. Boston: Printed for the Trustees, 1931.

HOFFMAN, WERNER. *Wilhelm Lehmbruck*. New York: Universe Books, Inc., 1959.

HOLLAND, LEICESTER B. "The Folger Shakespeare Library," *American Magazine of Art,* March, 1932.

HUSSEY, CHRISTOPHER. *Tait McKenzie: A Sculptor of Youth*. London: Country Life Ltd., 1929.

HUTTINGER, EDUARD. *Degas*. New York: Crown Publishers, Inc., 1960.

HUYGHE, RENÉ. *Art and the Spirit of Man*. New York: Harry N. Abrams, Inc., 1962.

_____. *Larousse Encyclopedia of Byzantine and Medieval Art*. New York: Prometheus Press, 1963.

_____. *Larousse Encyclopedia of Modern Art from 1800 to the Present Day*. New York: Prometheus Press, 1961.

_____. *Larousse Encyclopedia of Prehistoric and Ancient Art.* New York: Prometheus Press, 1957.

_____. *Larousse Encyclopedia of Renaissance and Baroque Art.* New York: Prometheus Press, 1958.

INDIA, GOVERNMENT OF. *The Way of the Buddha.* Delhi: Ministry of Information and Broadcasting, 1957.

JANSON, H. W. *Key Monuments of the History of Art.* New York: Harry N. Abrams, Inc., 1959.

_____, AND DORA JANE. *The Story of Painting: from Cave Painting to Modern Times.* New York: Harry N. Abrams, Inc., 1966.

JOHNSTON, AMES, "Waldmüller and His Paintings," *The American-German Review,* June, 1939.

JOOSTEN, ELLEN. *The Kröller-Müller Museum.* New York: Shorewood Publishing Co., Inc., 1965.

KENT, ROCKWELL. *Rockwellkentiana.* With a list of prints by Carl Zigrosser. New York: Harcourt, Brace and Company, 1933.

KETCHUM, RICHARD M. (ed.). *The Horizon Book of the Renaissance.* New York: American Heritage Publishing Co., Inc., 1961.

KNOWLTON, HELEN MARY. *Art-Life of William Morris Hunt.* Boston: Little, Brown & Co., 1899.

KULTERMANN, UDO. *The New Sculpture: Environments and Assemblages.* New York: Frederick A. Praeger, Inc., 1968.

LAKE, CARLTON, AND MAILLARD, ROBERT (eds.). *Dictionary of Modern Painting.* New York: Tudor Publishing Company, 1964.

LARKIN, OLIVER W. *Art and Life in America.* New York: Rinehart and Company, 1947.

LEVINSON-LESSING, V. E. *The Hermitage, Leningrad: Medieval and Renaissance Masters.* London: Paul Hamlyn, 1967.

LEVY, MERVYN. *The Human Form in Art.* London: Odhams Ltd., 1961.

LEYMARIE, JEAN. *Corot.* Translated by Stuart Gilbert. Geneva: Albert Skira, 1966.

LICHT, FRED. *Sculpture of the 19th and 20th Centuries.* Greenwich, Connecticut: New York Graphic Society Publishers, Ltd., 1967.

LOMBARDO, J. V. *Attilio Piccirilli: Life of an American Sculptor.* New York: Pitman Publishing Corporation, 1944.

LOS ANGELES COUNTY MUSEUM OF ART. *Gaston Lachaise 1882–1935: Sculpture and Drawings,* 1963.

_____. *Masterworks of Mexican Art: from pre-Columbian times to the present,* 1963.

McCOMB, ARTHUR. *Agnolo Bronzino: His Life and Works.* Cambridge, Massachusetts: Harvard University Press, 1928.

McKAY, WILLIAM, AND ROBERTS, W. *John Hoppner, R.A.* London: George Bell & Sons, 1909.

MacNEIL, HERMON A. "Small Bronzes," *American Magazine of Art (Art and Progress),* March, 1913.

McSPADDEN, J. WALKER. *Famous Painters of America.* New York: Thomas Y. Crowell Company, 1907.

MACK, GERSTLE. *Toulouse-Lautrec.* New York: Alfred A. Knopf, Inc., 1938.

MACLAGAN, ERIC. *Italian Sculpture of the Renaissance.* Cambridge, Massachusetts: Harvard University Press, 1935.

Magazine of Art, May, 1937.

MALITSKAYA, K. M. *Great Paintings from the Pushkin Museum.* New York: Harry N. Abrams, Inc., 1964.

MARTIN, W. *Dutch Painting of the Great Period 1650–1697.* Translated by D. Horning. London: B. T. Batsford Ltd., 1951.

MENDEOWITZ, DANIEL M. *Drawing.* New York: Holt, Rinehart & Winston, Inc., 1967.

MERYMAN, RICHARD. *Andrew Wyeth.* Boston: Houghton Mifflin Company, 1968.

MITTEN, DAVID GORDON, and DOERINGER, SUZANNAH F. *Master Bronzes from the Classical World.* Cambridge, Massachusetts: Fogg Art Museum, 1967.

MONGAN, AGNES (ed.). *One Hundred Master Drawings.* Cambridge, Massachusetts: Harvard University Press, 1949.

MØRK, POUL. *African Art.* Translated by Douglas Holmes. Copenhagen: Rhodos, 1967.

MOSKOWITZ, IRA (ed.). *Great Drawings of All Time.* 4 vols. New York: Shorewood Publishing Co., Inc., 1962.

MUKERJEE, RADHAKAMAL. *The Flowering of Indian Art.* London: Asia Publishing House, 1964.

MURRAY, PETER AND LINDA. *Dictionary of Art and Artists.* New York: Frederick A. Praeger, Inc., 1965.

MUSEUM OF MODERN ART, THE. *Alberto Giacometti.* New York, 1965.

————. *Gaston Lachaise: Retrospective Exhibition, January 30–March 7, 1935.* New York: 1935.

MYERS, BERNARD S. (ed.). *Encyclopedia of Painting.* New York: Crown Publishers, Inc., 1955.

————. *The German Expressionists: A Generation in Revolt.* New York: Frederick A. Praeger, Inc., 1957.

————. *Modern Art in the Making.* New York: McGraw-Hill Book Company, Inc., 1959.

NICOLSON, BENEDICT. *Hendrick Terbrugghen.* London: Lund Humphries & Co. Ltd., 1958.

NORMAN, JANE AND THEODORE. *Traveler's Guide to Europe's Art.* New York: Appleton-Century, 1965.

NOVOTNÝ, VLADIMIR. *Treasures of the Prague National Gallery.* London: Batchworth Press, 1960.

PANOFSKY, ERWIN. *Albrecht Dürer.* Vols. 1 and 2. Princeton, New Jersey: Princeton University Press, 1948.

PARKE, ROBERT ALLERTON. "A Petit-Maître of the Eighteenth Century," *International Studio,* July, 1927.

PARKER, KARL THEODORE. *The Drawings of Antoine Watteau.* London: B. T. Batsford Ltd., 1931.

PARROT, ANDRÉ. *Sumar: The Dawn of Art.* New York: Golden Press, 1961.

PEARSON, RALPH M. *The Modern Renaissance in American Art.* New York: Harper & Brothers, 1954.

PENROSE, ROLAND. *Picasso: His Life and Work.* New York: Harper & Brothers, 1958.

PIERACCI, EUGENIO. *Catalogue of the Royal Uffizi Gallery.* Florence, 1906.

POPE-HENNESSY, JOHN. *Italian High Renaissance and Baroque Sculpture.* London: Phaidon Publishers, Inc., 1963.

POPHAM, ARTHUR E. *Correggio's Drawings.* London: Oxford University Press. 1957.

PORTER, FAIRFIELD. *Thomas Eakins.* New York: George Braziller, Inc., 1959.

POST, CHANDLER RATHFON. *A History of Spanish Painting.* XIV: The Later Renaissance in Castile. Cambridge, Massachusetts: Harvard University Press, 1966.

POULSEN, VAGN HAGER. *Danish Painting and Sculpture.* Copenhagen: Det Danske Selskab, 1955.

RAGGHIANTI, CARLO LUDOVICO. *Giacomo Manzù: Sculptor.* Milan: Edizioni Del Milione, 1957.

READ, HERBERT. *The Art of Sculpture.* New York: Pantheon Books, 1956.

————. *A Concise History of Modern Sculpture.* London: Thames and Hudson Ltd., 1964.

REWALD, JOHN. *Giacomo Manzù.* Greenwich, Connecticut: New York Graphic Society Publishers, Ltd., 1967.

RICHARDSON, EDGAR PRESTON. *Washington Allston: A Study of the Romantic Artist in America.* Chicago: University of Chicago Press, 1948.

RICHTER, GISELA M. A. *Attic Red-Figured Vases: a Survey.* Revised edition. New Haven, Connecticut: Yale University Press, 1958.

————. *A Handbook of Greek Art.* London: Phaidon Press, 1939.

_____. *The Sculpture and Sculptors of the Greeks.* New revised edition. New Haven: Yale University Press, 1950.

RITCHIE, ANDREW CARNDUFF. *Aristide Maillol.* Buffalo, New York: Albright Art Gallery, 1945.

_____. *Sculpture of the Twentieth Century.* New York: The Museum of Modern Art, 1952.

ROBB, DAVID M. *The Harper History of Painting.* New York: Harper & Brothers, 1951.

_____, AND GARRISON, J. J. *Art in the Western World.* Third edition. New York: Harper & Brothers, 1953.

ROGERS, MEYRIC R. *Carl Milles: An Interpretation of His Work.* New Haven, Connecticut: Yale University Press, 1940.

ROSE, BARBARA. *American Art Since 1900.* New York: Frederick A. Praeger, Inc., 1967.

ROTHENSTEIN, JOHN. *The Tate Gallery.* New York: Harry N. Abrams, Inc., 1958.

ROUSSELL, AAGE (ed.). *The National Museum of Denmark.* Copenhagen: Nationalmuseet, 1957.

ROWLAND, BENJAMIN. *The Art and Architecture of India.* London: Penguin Books, 1953.

ROYAL ONTARIO MUSEUM. *Bulletin.* Toronto: University of Toronto, December, 1957.

RUHMER, EBERHARD. *Cranach.* Translated by Joan Spencer. London: Phaidon Publishers, 1963.

RUSSELL, ARCHIBALD GEORGE B. *Drawings by Guercino.* London: Edward Arnold & Co., 1923.

SACHS, PAUL J. *Modern Prints and Drawings.* New York: Alfred A. Knopf, Inc., 1954.

SALVINI, ROBERTO. *Modern Italian Sculpture.* New York: Harry N. Abrams, Inc., 1962.

SANDLER, IRVING. *Paul Burlin.* New York: The American Federation of Arts, 1962.

SCHMECKEBIER, LAURENCE E. *Modern Mexican Art.* Minneapolis, Minnesota: The University of Minnesota Press, 1939.

SCHMUTZLER, ROBERT. *Art Nouveau.* New York: Harry N. Abrams, Inc., 1962.

SCHÖNBERGER, ARNO; SOEHNER, HALLDOR; AND MÜLLER, THEODOR. *The Rococo Age: Art and Civilization of the 18th Century.* New York: McGraw-Hill Book Company, Inc., 1960.

Sculpture of Gaston Lachaise, The. New York: The Eakins Press, 1967.

Scultura e disegno: Artisti italiani contemporanei. Milan: Palazzo della Permanente, 1961.

SEATON-SCHMIDT, ANNA. "Frank W. Benson," *American Magazine of Art, The,* November, 1921.

SELZ, JEAN. *Modern Sculpture: Origins and Evolution.* Translated by Annette Michelson. New York: George Braziller, Inc., 1963.

SELZ, PETER. *German Expressionist Painting.* Berkeley, California: University of California Press, 1957.

_____. *New Images of Man.* New York: The Museum of Modern Art, 1959.

SERULLAZ, MAURICE. *French Drawings from Prud'hon to Daumier.* Greenwich, Connecticut: New York Graphic Society Publishers, Ltd., 1966.

SETA, ALESSANDRO DELLA. *Il Nudo Nell'Arte.* Milan: Bestetti & Tumminelli, 1930.

SEUPHOR, MICHEL. *The Sculpture of This Century.* New York: George Braziller, Inc., 1960.

SEWALL, JOHN IVES. *A History of Western Art.* New York: Holt, Rinehart & Winston, Inc., 1963.

SHEARMAN, JOHN. *Andrea del Sarto.* Vols. 1 and 2. Oxford, England: Oxford University Press, 1965.

SIVARAMAMURTI, C. *Indian Sculpture.* Indian Council for Cultural Relations. Bombay: Allied Publishers Private Ltd., 1961.

SLUSSER, JEAN PAUL. *Bernard Karfiol.* New York: Whitney Museum of American Art, 1931.

SOBY, JAMES THRALL. *Tchelitchew: Paintings, Drawings.* New York: The Museum of Modern Art, 1942.

SPELIOS, THOMAS. *Pictorial History of Greece.* New York: Crown Publishers, Inc., 1967.

STARKWEATHER, WILLIAM E. B. *Joaquín Sorolla: The Man and His Work.* Vol. 2: *Eight Essays on Joaquín Sorolla y Bastida.* New York: The Hispanic Society of America, 1909.

STECHOW, WOLFGANG. *Dutch Landscape Painting of the Seventeenth Century.* London: The Phaidon Press Ltd., 1966.

STERLING, CHARLES. *Great French Painting in the Hermitage.* New York: Harry N. Abrams, Inc., 1958.

STEWART, VIRGINIA. *45 Contemporary Mexican Artists.* Stanford, California: Stanford University Press, 1951.

STOUT, GEORGE L. *Treasures from the Isabella Stewart Gardner Museum.* New York: Crown Publishers, Inc., 1969.

STRUTT, EDWARD C. *Fra Filippo Lippi.* London: George Bell and Sons, 1901.

SYLVESTER, DAVID (ed.). *Henry Moore.* London: Percy Lund, Humphries & Company Ltd., 1957.

SYPHER, WYLIE. *Rococo to Cubism in Art and Literature.* New York: Random House, Inc., 1960.

TANNENBAUM, LIBBY. *James Ensor.* New York: The Museum of Modern Art, 1951.

Thorvaldsen's Museum. Copenhagen: G. E. C. Gad, 1926.

TIETZE, HANS. *The Drawings of the Venetian Painters in the 15th and 16th Centuries.* New York: J. J. Augustin Publishers, 1944.

——. *European Master Drawings in the United States.* New York: J. J. Augustin Publishers, 1947.

——. *Masterpieces of European Painting in America.* New York: Oxford University Press, 1939.

——, AND TIETZE-CONRAT, E. *Drawings of Venetian Painters of the 15th and 16th Centuries.* New York: J. J. Augustin Publishers, 1944.

TIETZE-CONRAT, E. *Mantegna: Paintings, Drawings, Engravings.* London: Phaidon Press, 1955.

TRAPIER, ELIZABETH DU GUÉ. *Ribera.* New York: The Hispanic Society of America, 1952.

UPJOHN, EVERARD M.; WINGERT, PAUL S.; AND MAHLER, JANE GASTON. *History of World Art.* New York: Oxford University Press, Inc., 1958.

VAN DYKE, JOHN C. *American Painting and Its Tradition.* New York: Charles Scribner's Sons, 1919.

THE VASARI SOCIETY FOR THE REPRODUCTION OF DRAWINGS BY OLD MASTERS. Second series, Part IV, Oxford, England, 1923.

VOLAVKA, VOJTĚCH. *French Paintings and Engravings of the XIXth Century in Czechoslovakia.* Prague: Artia, 1954.

WALKER, JOHN, AND MACGILL, JAMES. *Great American Paintings from Smibert to Bellows 1729–1924.* New York: Oxford University Press, 1943.

WECHSLER, HERMAN J. *Great Prints and Printmakers.* New York: Harry N. Abrams, Inc., 1967.

WERNER, ALFRED. *Amedeo Modigliani.* New York: Harry N. Abrams, Inc., 1966.

WHEELER, MONROE. *Soutine.* New York: The Museum of Modern Art, 1950.

WITTKOWER, RUDOLF. *Art and Architecture in Italy 1600–1750.* Baltimore, Maryland: Penguin Books, Inc., 1958.

WOLDERING, IRMGARD. *Gods, Men & Pharaohs: The Glory of Egyptian Art.* New York: Harry N. Abrams, Inc., 1967.

WOLF, ROBERT ERICH, AND MILLEN, RONALD. *Renaissance and Mannerist Art.* New York: Harry N. Abrams, Inc., 1968.

YARROW, WILLIAM, AND BOUCHE, LOUIS. *Robert Henri: His Life and Works.* New York: Boni and Liveright, 1921.

ZIBRANDTSEN, JAN. *Moderne Dansk Maleri.* Copenhagen: Gyldendal, 1967.

ZIMMER, HEINRICH. *The Art of Indian Asia.* Vols. 1 and 2. New York: Pantheon Books, 1955.

INDEX

Numerals indicate pages on which illustrations appear.